INTERVIEWING
AS QUALITATIVE RESEARCH

A Guide for Researchers
in Education and the Social Sciences

I. E. SEIDMAN

Teachers College, Columbia University
New York and London

Published by Teachers College Press, 1234 Amsterdam Avenue
New York, NY 10027

Library of Congress Cataloging-in-Publication Data

Seidman, I. E.
    Interviewing as qualitative research : a guide for researchers in
education and the social sciences / I.E. Seidman.
        p. cm.
    Includes bibliographical references and index.
    ISBN 0-8077-3074-2
        1. Interviewing.   2. Social sciences — Research — Methodology.
    3. Education — Research — Methodology.   I. Title.
    H61.28.S45   1991   90-28645
    300'.723 — dc20   CIP

Printed on acid-free paper

Manufactured in the United States of America

98   97   96   8   7   6   5   4

Contents

Preface

In my experience as a teacher, I have worked with many graduate students who have deep and passionate interests they wish to pursue in their dissertations. Often, however, they are stymied by the lack of an appropriate and feasible methodology. They are, in Sartre's (1968) terms, "in search of a method."

This book is intended for doctoral candidates who are engaged in that search and who think that in-depth interviewing might be appropriate for them and their research topic. It will also serve more experienced researchers who, interested in qualitative research, may be turning to the possibilities of interviewing for the first time. Finally, the book is geared to professors in search of a supplementary text on in-depth interviewing that connects method and technique with broader issues of qualitative research. For both individuals and classes, the book provides a step-by-step introduction to the research process using in-depth interviewing. Within the text, I suggest a practice project and steps that allow the readers to study their own interviewing practice.

The text centers on a phenomenological approach to in-depth interviewing. The Introduction outlines how I came to do interviewing research. Chapter 1 discusses a rationale for using interviewing as a research method and the potential of narratives as ways of knowing. Chapter 2 presents a structure for in-depth, phenomenologically based interviewing that I and my associates have used in our research projects. The text provides specific guidance on how to carry out this approach to interviewing and the principles of adapting it to one's own goals. Chapter 3 explores issues that may make proposal writing daunting and discusses meaningful but simple questions that can guide the researcher through the process. Chapter 4, stressing pitfalls and snares to avoid in the process, discusses issues in establishing access, making contact with, and selecting participants. Chapter 5 examines the issue of "informed consent" and shows how its ethical obligations have methodological benefits. Chapter 6 avoids a cookbook approach but discusses specific interviewing skills and techniques and links them to important issues in interviewing and qualitative research. The chapter stresses how to listen as well as how to ask questions. Chapter 7 explores interviewing as a relationship, places that relationship within the context of the issues of class, race, and gender, and stresses equity as the necessary element in interviewing relationships. Chapter 8 discusses how to manage, work with, and share the vast amount of data generated in in-depth interviewing. It guides the reader through a process of reducing the materials and sharing the results with a wider audience in narrative profiles and discussions of themes that emerge from the interviews.

While proposing a phenomenological approach to in-depth interviewing, the book provides and discusses principles and methods that can be adapted to a range of approaches. Throughout the text I have provided examples from interviews done by me, my colleagues, and graduate students that illustrate the issues under discussion. I try to maintain a balance between sharing my experience with in-depth interviewing so that a reader can use what he or she may, and giving enough explicit guidance so that a reader can successfully conceptualize and carry out a research project based on the approach described.

In addition, I describe a practice project that individuals or classes can use to gain concrete experience with the method in a short amount of time. My goal has been to write a text short and clear enough to provide useful guidance to the individual researcher about in-depth interviewing as a research methodology and at the same time to connect that method to broader issues in qualitative research. Therefore, I have placed the text in the context of others' work on interviewing and issues in qualitative research. Through the references I cite, I have suggested supplementary reading to enable the reader to go beyond this text. Although the examples cited in the book are taken from the field of education, and throughout I have thought of researchers in education as my primary audience, all those interested in in-depth interviewing as a research method can draw from the text.

ACKNOWLEDGMENTS

Writing a book takes place in the context of a life. This book has been percolating in my mind since 1982, and the people I mention below have all been connected to my writing it. In each case there is a story, little of which, except my appreciation of their contributions, can be told here. In earlier work I did with Patrick Sullivan and Mary Bray Schatzkamer, we wrote a report for the National Institute of Education. For that report, I wrote a chapter called "What We Have Learned About In-Depth, Phenomenological Interviewing," which I began to circulate to doctoral students who became interested in the method, especially to those who worked with me in our seminar, In-Depth Interviewing and Issues in Qualitative Research. I want to thank all the graduate students who have worked with me over the years in that seminar and who through their work and our discussions have contributed to this text. Special thanks to Karen Burke, Linda Miller-Cleary, Sylvia Galvan, Chris Hardin, James O'Donnell, Sharon Santilli, Mary Bray Schatzkamer, Marguerite Sheehan, Antonia Tingitana, Beatrice Tremblay, Ronna Tulgen, Kay Williamson, Sherry Woods, Mary Alice Wolf, and Sally Young, present and former doctoral candidates whose interviewing work has informed and illuminated this text.

I was lucky to have Elizabeth Dichter as a research assistant for this book. What a pleasure it is to work with a person who anticipates — is always half a step ahead in the process — and is seldom satisfied with anything less than excellence in her work. She also did extensive background work for Chapter 5. Mary Bray Schatzkamer once again contributed her thoughtfulness about interviewing by culling pages of transcripts to identify examples of interviewing techniques for Chapter 6. To them, Jun-Chih Lin, Chuck Rice, and to Donna Lalond for responding to every single question and request I had about computers, my appreciation.

Over the past 10 years, we have carried out much of our interviewing work with the support of the Exxon Foundation, the former National Institute of Education, and the Fund for the Improvement of Post Secondary Education. I am grateful to these agencies and their officers, especially John Wirt, Clifford Adelman, and Jaymie Lewis for seeing the possibility of in-depth interviewing for both research and evaluating purposes. My thanks also to Marilyn Haring-Hidore, dean of our School of Education at the University of Massachusetts/Amherst, David Bloome, head of my division, and Stan Scarpati and Connie Bunker of our Office of Research, who have been consistent in their support of the work that has led to this text.

My appreciation to my colleague Richard J. Clark who, as director of our Math/English/Science and Technology Teacher Education Program, gave me the opportunity to further my work with interviewing methodology, and to Helen Schneider, Peter Cannone, and the student teachers and mentors at our East Longmeadow, Holyoke, and Greenfield clinical sites who also supported the extension of our interviewing research. John Booss, Pat Dodds, Sylvia Forman, Austra Gaige, Atron Gentry, Christopher Hurn, Elizabeth Keitel, Seth Kreisberg, Sari and George Lipkin, Barbara Love, Robert Maloy, Ken Parker, Agni Saucier, Judy Solsken, Virginia Vincenti, and Gerald Weinstein, friends and present and former colleagues, each contributed, sometimes knowingly and sometimes unknowingly, to the writing of this book. I appreciate what they have offered to me.

Teresa Barton, Janice Dore, Louise Gaudet, Patricia S. Griffin, Lawrence F. Locke, and Judith H. Miller each read a draft of the manuscript. I imposed upon them at the end of a busy semester. I deeply valued and learned from their detailed, insightful, and timely responses. My appreciation, also, to Sarah J. Biondello, Cathy McClure, Karen Altman, and especially the late Ron Galbraith of Teachers College Press, all of whom encouraged and nurtured the development of this book.

Our daughter Rachel sent me the Todorov book and other materials from her study of American history. She saw connections to interviewing in her reading that broadened my perspective. Our son, Ethan, himself a lucid writer, is also an insightful reader and a trenchant responder to my writing. Throughout his senior year in college, I sent him drafts of each of my chapters. I also gave drafts to my wife, Linda. They would each edit, then blend their comments, and return the chapters to me for further work. Without their clarity and facility with language and ideas, this book would have been less than it is. In the final stages of the work, my mother-in-law, Ruth Levenson, pitched in with zest and care. I loved sharing my work with them, learning from their responses, and I treasure our daughter and son's becoming my colleagues in this effort, along with my partner, my wife.

This book gives me the opportunity to express a lifetime of appreciation to certain of my teachers still present and to the memories of others: Miss Fox, Miss Blue, Mrs. Stahl, Mrs. Stark, Mrs. Prusa, N. C. Davis, Dr. Dilley, Leonard Hoffman, Andrew Bongiorno, George Goethals, Edwin Sauer, Elizabeth Cohen, and Alfred Grommon. Finally, my appreciation to Edward W. Hughes, Jr., who taught me most of what I have learned about active listening, simple but deep questioning, and the difficulty and desirability of sometimes saying nothing. This book is dedicated to him.

Introduction: How I Came to Interviewing

In my study at home, I have a picture of my grandfather, whom I never met, on the bookshelf. He was born sometime around 1870 and he died in the early 1940s. In the sepia-tone photograph that I have, he is a bearded man with sad eyes, wearing a worn jacket over a sweater and tie. His eyes look out at me no matter where I am in the room.

Whenever I asked my father about his father, he said his father was a religious man. "What did he do?" I would ask, and my father would say, "He studied." I never got very much of his story. I know only that he was a religious man, that he studied, that he didn't do much else, that his family was poor, and that he died of a heart attack running away from the Germans early in World War II.

My father was an immigrant from Russia. He came to this country with my mother in 1921. While I was growing up in Cleveland, Ohio, and upon visits to my family home later, I asked my father about his experiences in Russia (my mother, also from Russia, died in 1963): What was it like to live there? How did he come to leave? I asked him about his family, about what it was like to be a child in Russia.

His reply, almost invariably, was, "Why do you want to know? We were poor. Everyone was poor. There was nothing there. America is wonderful. Why do you want to know about Russia?" My father died in 1989 and, although I have accumulated a few anecdotes about his days in Russia, I did not learn the story of his life there, and I never will.

After graduating from college, I earned an M.A.T. degree and taught English for 4½ years in every grade from 7 through 12. Perhaps it was as a teacher of English that I first came to see stories and the details of people's lives as a way of knowing and understanding. Why else was I teaching literature and writing if I didn't believe that?

To suggest that stories are a way to knowledge and understanding may not seem scholarly. When I was earning my doctorate in education in the mid-1960s, the faculty in my graduate program in teacher education seemed almost totally committed to building knowledge in education through experimentation. My graduate experience was governed by a sense that research in education could be as scientific as it was in the natural and physical sciences. Experimentalists informed by behaviorism dominated my graduate experience in research. I remember sitting in an advanced educational psychology class. The professor was discussing conditioning as a basis for understanding learning. It was a class of about 60, but discussion was officially encouraged. I raised my hand and said something about humans being different from rats because people had language. I don't remember exactly what the professor said in return, but it was not what I would call today a collaborative response.

That day brought to a culmination my feeling of being stifled and frustrated by behaviorism during the first year of my graduate study. Only of late have I come to appreciate a suggestion my doctoral advisor and mentor, Alfred Grommon, made to me: that I do a biography of one of the early presidents of the National Council of Teachers of English for my dissertation. At that time, I considered his suggestion well intended but somehow not connected to my interests. Now I realize that he may have been offering me a way out of the procrustean bed of behaviorism and experimentalism that pervaded my graduate experience.

Despite my aversions, I did an experimental dissertation. I designed a study of the effects on students' achievement motivation of teachers' comments on their writing. I had different treatment groups; I established independent variables and dependent variables; I enlisted a group of English teachers in the field to carry out "the treatments" that I had designed on "the subjects."

Nathan Gage's (1963) *Handbook of Research of Teaching* had recently been published. In some respects it was treated as a Bible in our graduate program. I remember reading and rereading, and developing mnemonic codes to help me remember the threats to validity and reliability described and analyzed in Campbell and Stanley's (1963) chapter on "Experimental and Quasi-Experimental Design for Research in Teaching."

While at the time I chafed under the heavy emphasis on experimentalism, I now respect how committed my graduate institution was to research in education. Despite my resistance to the approach then, I now realize how valuable and important it was for me to confront the assumptions of positivism and behaviorism that seemed to me to dominate the institution. In my thinking about both teaching and research, my professional career has been shaped by that confrontation. There were also, at the time, professors who provided an alternative point of view. They helped open my mind to exploring new intellectual paths, especially the impact of social and cultural forces on individual experience in education. In the end, my graduate school communicated a sense of imperative about research in education that has had a long-lasting effect on me for which I am grateful.

As I continued my career in education after I earned my doctorate in 1967, I took a position that left me confused about research. I joined the English department of the University of Washington as one of three faculty members in English education. I had surprisingly little contact with the College of Education as I began to face the pressures of publishing in my field. On some levels, I was estranged from my own dissertation because I had not really believed in its methodology, so I did not then and never have sought to publish an article based on it. That first and formative year, I did do some writing, but no research. I often wonder how I would have figured out my relationship to research if I had stayed at the University of Washington. Given my experimental experience, my discomfort with it, and my position as a teacher educator in a strong, conservative English department where the notion of research was that of literary scholarship, my research options at that time were not clear to me.

I stayed at the University of Washington only a year. I had a good position in an exceptionally strong department in a public university that was the pride of the Northwest; but I left in 1968 to become the assistant dean of the School of Education at the University of Massachusetts at Amherst under the leadership of Dwight Allen. This is not the place to dwell at length on that part of the story (Frenzy at UMass, 1970; Resnik, 1972). It looms larger in my mind, I am sure, than in most others'. Suffice it to say that our goal reflected the times and our sense of them. Our objective was to reform professional education and to have our School of Education play a role in making society more equitable. I will always respect the idealism of those goals. In our inexperience and naivete, we made many mistakes along the way — in and among some significant accomplishments. As the times changed, and our mistakes accumulated, a new administration was called for. I was a faculty member again after six intense years as an administrator. Although I learned much about higher education during my tenure as an administrator, I gained little new experience in doing research.

After my administrative years, I was fortunate enough to take a sabbatical in London with my family. I had the chance to do reading that would allow me to return responsibly to my teaching. In addition to reading works on the teaching of English, which I had been away from for 7 years, I read Thomas Kuhn's (1970) *The Structure of Scientific Revolution* and thought about my experience with science and research as a graduate student. I read that book just in time. When I got back to the States, references to "governing paradigms" in journal articles abounded.

Upon my return, I co-taught a course with Robert Woodbury on Leadership in Higher Education. A new faculty member by the name of David Schuman had joined our school in the area of higher education. Through my teaching in the Higher Education Program I came to know him. Of the many constitutive events that led me to interviewing as a research methodology, meeting and working with Schuman was the most significant. Because I had rejected the approach to research I had learned in graduate school and had not learned a new approach in my short time at Washington, nor in the 6 years I was an administrator, I was, paradoxically, a relatively experienced faculty member searching for a research methodology.

Schuman was beginning to write a book based on interviewing research that he had done with Kenneth Dolbeare. Schuman's book *Policy Analysis, Education, and Everyday Life* did not come out until 1982, but in the meantime he generously shared with me and Patrick Sullivan his methodological approach, which he called "phenomenological interviewing." He also directed me to some of the readings he had done in coming to the type of interviewing research he and Dolbeare had done. I remember in particular his suggesting to me that I read William James's (1947) *Essays in Radical Empiricism* and *In a Pluralistic Universe*, Sartre's (1968) *Search for a Method*, Matson's (1966) *The Broken Image*, and, most directly relevant, Alfred Schutz's (1967) *The Phenomenology of the Social World*.

I was ready for what Schuman was generously willing to share. I remember the feeling that I would like to do interviewing as a research method. I remember thinking what a good way it was to learn about people and schools as I listened to Schuman and began to build in my mind upon what he was saying. Additionally, I had had experience with psychotherapy. Through that process, I learned to appreciate even further the importance of language and stories in a person's life as ways toward knowing and understanding. That personal experience made me even more ready to consider interviewing as a research method.

Sullivan and I were co-teaching a course for community college teachers on critical issues in community college teaching. Sullivan, with his colleague, Judithe Speidel, had earlier done a documentary film on the Shakers (*The Shaker Legacy*, 1976), and we decided now to do a film on teaching in community colleges based on the interviewing method we had learned from Schuman. We received a grant from the Exxon Corporation to support our interviewing 25 community college teachers on how they came to teaching, what it was like for them, and what it meant to them.

The film was produced in 1982, and we then received a second grant from the National Institute of Education (NIE) to expand our interviewing to community college faculty in California and New York. The work continued to be a deeply satisfying way to do research. I loved talking with people about their work as faculty members and learning about community college education through the experience of those who taught there. We interviewed a total of 76 community college faculty and, through the efforts of Mary Bray Schatzkamer, 24 students to try to gain an understanding of what it was like to work and teach in a community college. That interviewing led to a draft of a manuscript called "What We Have Learned About In-Depth Interviewing" that was published as Chapter 14 of our Final Report to NIE (Seidman, Sullivan, & Schatzkamer, 1983), and a book on community college teaching called *In the Words of the Faculty* (Seidman, 1985).

While doing our research on community college faculty, Sullivan and I began to co-teach a graduate seminar, In-Depth Interviewing and Issues in Qualitative Work. I continue to teach that seminar and to do interviewing research, now focusing on interviewing student and first-year teachers and their mentors on the experience of becoming a teacher and being a mentor. That work has been as part of a research and evaluation effort on our Math/Education/Science and Technology Teacher Education Program and our East Longmeadow/University of Massachusetts Clinical Site Teacher Education Program, both supported by grants from the Fund for the Improvement of Post Secondary Education. (See Clark & Seidman, 1988; O'Donnell, Schneider, Seidman, & Tingitana, 1989.)

Interviewing the community college teachers was the first research I had done that was neither literary nor experimental. I had finally found a way to do "empirical" work that was emotionally and intellectually satisfying. In spite of problems and complications everywhere in the research process, from conceiving the idea and contacting participants to writing up the results of 3 years of interviewing, this kind of work was and continues to be deeply satisfying for me. It is hard and sometimes draining, but I have never lost the feeling that it is a privilege to gather the stories of people through interviewing and to come to understand their experience through their stories. Sharing those stories through de-

veloping profiles of the people I had interviewed in their own words and
making thematic connections among their experiences proved to be a
fruitful way of working with the material and of writing about what I
had learned. A good deal of what follows is an attempt to describe and
explain the roots of the intellectual and emotional pleasure I have gained
from interviewing as a research method in education.

One final introductory note: Although this book concentrates on
in-depth interviewing as a method of research in education, I am not
proposing it as the sole, or the best, method of doing research. Some
scholars argue that having multiple sources of data is one of the intrinsic
characteristics of qualitative research (see Patton, 1989). The interviewing method I describe, explain, and, hope, illuminate can be done in
combination with other approaches to understanding the world outside
ourselves. On the other hand, I think a case can be made that in some
research situations the in-depth interview, as the primary and perhaps
singular method of investigation, is most appropriate. Use of in-depth
interviews alone, when done with skill, can avoid tensions that sometimes
arise when a researcher uses multiple methods. That is especially the case
when those methods may be based on different assumptions of what it
means to understand the experience of others.

1

Why Interview

I interview because I am interested in other people's stories. Most simply put, stories are a way of knowing. The root of the word *story* is the Greek word *histor*, which means one who is "wise" and "learned" (Watkins, 1985, p. 74). Telling stories is essentially a meaning-making process. When people tell stories, they select details of their experience from their stream of consciousness. Every whole story, Aristotle tells us, has a beginning, a middle, and an end (Butcher, 1902). In order to give the details of their experience a beginning, middle, and end, people must reflect on their experience. It is this process of selecting constitutive details of experience, reflecting on them, giving them order, and thereby making sense of them that makes telling stories a meaning-making experience. (See Schutz, 1967, p. 12 and p. 50, for aspects of the relationship between reflection and meaning making.)

Every word that people use in telling their stories is a microcosm of their consciousness (Vygotsky, 1987, pp. 236–237). Individuals' consciousness gives access to the most complicated social and educational issues, because social and educational issues are abstractions based on the concrete experience of people. W. E. B. Du Bois knew this when he wrote, "I seem to see a way of elucidating the inner meaning of life and significance of that race problem by explaining it in terms of the one human life that I know best" (Wideman, 1990, p. xiv).

Although anthropologists have long been interested in people's stories as a way of understanding their culture, such an approach to research in education has not been widely accepted. For many years those who were trying to make education a respected academic discipline in universities argued that education could be a science (Bailyn, 1963). They urged their colleagues in education to adapt research models patterned after those in the natural and physical sciences.

In the 1970s a reaction to the dominance of experimental, quantita-

1

tive, and behaviorist research in education began to develop (Gage, 1989). The critique had its own energy and was also a reflection of the era's more general resistance to received authority (Gitlin, 1987, esp. chap. 4). Researchers in education split into two, almost warring, camps: quantitative and qualitative.

It is interesting to note the debate between the two camps got especially fierce and the polemics more extreme when the economics of higher education took a downturn in the mid-1970s and early 1980s (Gage, 1989). But the political battles were informed by real epistemological differences. The underlying assumptions about the nature of reality, the relationship of the knower and the known, the possibility of objectivity, the possibility of generalization, inherent in each approach are different and to a considerable degree contradictory. To begin to understand these basic differences in assumptions, I urge you to read James (1947), chapter 1 of Lincoln and Guba (1985), Mannheim (1975), and Polanyi (1958).

For those interested in interviewing as a method of research, perhaps the most telling argument between the two camps centers on the significance of language to inquiry with human beings. Bertaux (1981) has argued that those who urge educational researchers to imitate the natural sciences seem to ignore one basic difference between the subjects of inquiry in the natural sciences and those in the social sciences: The subjects of inquiry in the social sciences can talk and think. Unlike a star, or a chemical, or a lever, "If given a chance to talk freely, people appear to know a lot about what is going on" (p. 39).

At the very heart of what it means to be human is the ability of people to symbolize their experience through language. To understand human behavior means to understand the use of language (Heron, 1981). Heron points out that the original and archetypal paradigm of human inquiry is two persons talking and asking questions of each other. He says,

> The use of language, itself, . . . contains within it the paradigm of cooperative inquiry; and since language is the primary tool whose use enables human construing and intending to occur, it is difficult to see how there can be any more fundamental mode of inquiry for human beings into the human condition. (p. 26)

Interviewing, then, is a basic mode of inquiry. Recounting narratives of experience has been the major way throughout recorded history that humans have made sense of their experience. To those who would ask, however, "Is telling stories science?" Peter Reason (1981) would respond,

Goal

The best stories are those which stir people's minds, hearts, and souls and by so doing give them new insights into themselves, their problems and their human condition. The challenge is to develop a human science that can more fully serve this aim. The question then, is not "Is story telling science?" but "Can science learn to tell good stories?" (p. 50)

THE PURPOSE OF INTERVIEWING

The purpose of in-depth interviewing is not to get answers to questions, nor to test hypotheses, and not to "evaluate" as the term is normally used. (See Patton, 1989, for an exception.) At the root of in-depth interviewing is an interest in understanding the experience of other people and the meaning they make of that experience.

Being interested in others is the key to some of the basic assumptions underlying interviewing technique. It requires that we interviewers keep our egos in check. It requires that we realize we are not the center of the world. It demands that our actions as interviewers indicate that others' stories are important.

At the heart of interviewing research is an interest in other individuals' stories because they are of worth. That is why people whom we interview are hard to code with numbers, and why finding pseudonyms for participants[1] is a complex and sensitive task. Their stories defy the anonymity of a number and almost that of a pseudonym. To hold the conviction that we know enough already and don't need to know others' stories is not only anti-intellectual; it also leaves us, at one extreme, prone to violence to others (Todorov, 1984).

Schutz (1967, chap. 3) offers us guidance. First of all, he says that it is never possible to understand another perfectly, because to do so would mean that we had entered into the other's stream of consciousness and experienced what he or she had. If we could do that, we would *be* that other person.

Recognizing the limits on our understanding of others, we can still strive to comprehend them by understanding their actions. Schutz gives the example of walking in the woods and seeing a man chopping wood. The observer can watch this behavior and have an "observational understanding" of the woodchopper. But what the observer understands as a result of this observation may not be at all consistent with how the woodchopper views his own behavior. (In analogous terms, think of the problem of observing students or teachers.) To understand the woodchopper's behavior, the observer would have to gain access to the woodchopper's "subjective understanding," that is, know what meaning he himself made out of his chopping wood. The way to meaning, Schutz says, is to be able to put behavior in context. Was the woodchopper chopping wood to supply a logger, heat his home, or get in shape? (For Schutz's complete and detailed explication of this argument, see esp. chaps. 1–3.)

Interviewing provides access to the context of people's behavior and thereby provides a way for researchers to understand the meaning of that behavior. A basic assumption in in-depth interviewing research is that the meaning people make of their experience affects the way they carry out that experience. To observe a teacher, student, principal, or counselor provides access to their behavior. Interviewing allows us to put behavior in context and provides access to understanding their action. The best article I have read on the importance of context for meaning is Elliot Mishler's (1979) "Meaning in Context: Is There Any Other Kind?" the theme of which was later expanded into his book, *Research Interviewing: Context and Narrative* (1986).

INTERVIEWING: THE METHOD OR A METHOD?

The primary way a researcher can investigate an educational organization, institution, or process is through the experience of the individual people, the "others" who make up the organization or carry out the process. Social abstractions like "education" are best understood through the experiences of the individuals whose work and lives are the stuff upon which the abstractions are built (Ferrarotti, 1981). So much research is done on schooling in the United Sates; yet so little of it is based on studies involving the perspective of the students, teachers, administrators, counselors, special subject teachers, nurses, psychologists, cafeteria workers, secretaries, school crossing guards, bus drivers, parents, and school committee members, whose individual and collective experience constitutes schooling.

A researcher can approach the experience of people in contemporary organizations through examining personal and institutional documents, through observation, through exploring history, through experimentation, through questionnaires and surveys, and through a review of existing literature. If the researcher's goal, however, is to understand the meaning people involved in education make of their experience, then interviewing provides a necessary, if not always completely sufficient, avenue of inquiry.

An educational researcher might suggest that the other avenues of inquiry listed above offer access to people's experience and the meaning they make of it as effectively as and at less cost than does interviewing. I would not argue that there is one right way, or that one way is better than another. Howard Becker, Blanche Geer, and Martin Trow carried on an argument in 1957 that still gains attention in the literature because, among other reasons, Becker and Geer seemed to be arguing that participant observation was the single and best way to gather data about people in society. Trow took exception and argued back that for some purposes interviewing is far superior (Becker & Geer, 1957; Trow, 1957).

The adequacy of a research method depends on the purpose of the research and the questions being asked (Locke, 1989). If a researcher is asking a question such as, "How do people behave in this classroom?" then participant observation might be the best method of inquiry. If the researcher is asking, "How does the placement of students in a level of the tracking system correlate with social class and race?" then a survey may be the best approach. If the researcher is wondering whether a new curriculum affects students' achievements on standardized tests, then a quasi-experimental, controlled study might be most effective. Research interests don't always or often come out so neatly. In many cases, research interests have many levels, and as a result multiple methods may be appropriate. If the researcher is interested, however, in what it is like for students to be in the classroom, what their experience is, and what meaning they make out of that experience — if the interest is in what Schutz calls their "subjective understanding" — then it seems to me that interviewing, in most cases, may be the best avenue of inquiry.

I say most cases, because below a certain age, interviewing children may not work. I would not rule out the possibility, however, of sitting down with even very young children to ask them about their experience. Carlisle (1988) interviewed first-grade students about their responses to literature. She found that although she had to shorten the length of time that she interviewed students, she was successful at exploring with first graders their experience with books.

WHY NOT INTERVIEW?

Interviewing research takes a great deal of time and, sometimes, money. The researcher has to conceptualize the project, establish access and make contact with participants, interview them, transcribe the data, and then work with the material and share what he or she has learned. Sometimes I sense that a new researcher is choosing one method because he or she thinks it will be easier than another. Any method of inquiry worth anything takes time, thoughtfulness, energy, and money. But interviewing is especially labor intensive. If the researcher does not have the money or the support to hire secretarial help to transcribe tapes, it is his or her labor that is at stake. (See Chapter 8.)

Interviewing requires that researchers establish access to, and make contact with, potential participants whom they have never met. If they are unduly shy about themselves or hate to make phone calls, the process of getting started can be daunting. Of course, overcoming shyness, taking the initiative, establishing contact, and scheduling and completing the first set of interviews can be a very satisfying accomplishment.

My sense is that graduate programs today in general, and the one in which I teach in particular, are much more individualized and less monolithic than I thought them to be when I was a doctoral candidate. Students have a choice of the type of research methodology they wish to pursue. But in some graduate programs there may be a cost to pay for that freedom: Those interested in qualitative research may not be required to learn the tenets of what is called "quantitative" research. As a result, some students tend not to understand the history of the method they are using nor the critique of positivism and experimentalism out of which some approaches to qualitative research in education grew. (For those interested in learning that critique as an underpinning for their work, as a start see Johnson, 1975; Lincoln & Guba, 1985.)

Many graduate students I know do not really understand the so-called paradigm wars (Gage, 1989) that took place in the 1970s and 1980s and are still going on in the early 1990s. By not being aware of the history of the battle and the fields upon which it has been fought, students may not understand their own position in it and the potential implications for their careers as it continues. If doctoral candidates choose to use interviewing as a research methodology for their dissertation or other early research, they should know that their choice to do qualitative research is not the dominant one in the history of educational research. Although qualitative research has gained ground in the last 20 years, professional organizations and professional journals in education, and personnel committees on which senior faculty tend to sit, are often dominated by those who have a predilection for quantitative research. In some arenas, doctoral candidates choosing to do qualitative rather than quantitative research may have to fight a stiffer battle to establish themselves as credible. They may also have to be comfortable with being outside the center of the conventional educational establishments. They will have to learn to search out funding agencies, journals, and publishers open to qualitative approaches. (For a discussion of these interactions, see Mishler, 1986, esp. pp. 141–143.)

Although the choice of a research method ideally is determined by what one is trying to learn, those coming into the field of educational research must know that some researchers and scholars see the choice as a political and moral one. (See Bertaux, 1981; Fay, 1987; Gage, 1989; Lather, 1986a, 1986b; Popkowitz, 1984). The high moral road is often taken by those who espouse qualitative research. Among other criticism, they decry the way quantitative research turns human beings into numbers.

But, there are equally serious moral issues involved in qualitative research. As I read Todorov's (1984) *The Conquest of America*, I began to think of interviewing as a process that turns others into subjects so that their words can be appropriated for the benefit of the researcher. Daphne Patai (1987) raises a similar issue when she points out that the Brazilian women she interviewed seemed to enjoy the activity, but she was deeply troubled by the possibility that she was exploiting them for her scholarship.

Interviewing as exploitation is a serious concern and provides a contradiction and a tension within my work that I have not fully resolved. Part of the issue is, as Patai recognizes, an economic one. Steps can be taken to assure that participants receive an equitable share of whatever financial profits ensue from their participation in research. But at a deeper level, there is a more basic question of research for whom, by whom, and to what end. Research is often done by people in relative positions of power in the guise of reform. All too often the only interests served are those of the researcher's personal advancement. It is a constant struggle to make the research process equitable, especially in the United States where a good deal of our social structure is inequitable.

CONCLUSION

So why choose interviewing? Perhaps constitutive events in your life, as in mine, have added up to your being "interested" in interviewing as a method. It is a powerful way to gain insight into educational issues through understanding the experience of the individuals whose lives constitute education. As a method of inquiry, interviewing is most consistent with people's ability to make meaning through language. It affirms the importance of the individual without denigrating the possibility of community and collaboration. Finally, it is deeply satisfying to researchers who are interested in others' stories.

NOTE

1. The word a researcher chooses to refer to the person being interviewed often communicates important information about the researcher's purpose in interviewing and his or her view of the relationship. In the literature about interviewing a wide range of terms is used. *Interviewee* or *respondent* (Richardson, 1965; Lincoln & Guba, 1985) casts the participant in a passive role and the process of interviewing as one of giving answers to questions. Some writers refer to the person being interviewed as the *subject* (Patai, 1987). On one hand, this term can be seen as positive; it changes the person being interviewed from object to subject. On the other hand, the term *subject* implies that the interviewing relationship is hierarchical and that the person being interviewed can be subjugated. Alternatively, anthropologists tend to use the term *informant* (Ellen, 1984), because the people they interview inform them about a culture.

In searching for the term we wanted to use, my colleagues and I focused on the fact that in-depth interviewing encourages people to reconstruct their experience actively within the context of their lives. To reflect that active stance, we chose the word *participants* to refer to the people we interview. That word seems to capture both the sense of active involvement that occurs in an in-depth interview and the sense of equity that we try to build in our interviewing relationships.

2

A Structure for In-Depth, Phenomenological Interviewing

The word *interviewing* covers a wide range of practices. There are tightly structured, survey interviews with preset, standardized, normally closed questions. At the other end of the continuum are open-ended, apparently unstructured, anthropological interviews that might be seen almost, according to Spradley (1979), as friendly conversations. (For a description of the wide range of approaches to interviewing, see Bertaux, 1981; Briggs, 1986, p. 20; Ellen, 1984, p. 231; Lincoln & Guba, 1985, pp. 268–269; Mishler, 1986, pp. 14–15; Richardson, Dohrenwena, & Klein, 1965, pp. 36–40; and Spradley, 1979, pp. 57–58.)

This book, however, is about what I and my colleagues have come to call in-depth, phenomenologically based interviewing. The method combines life-history interviewing (see Bertaux, 1981) and focused, in-depth interviewing informed by assumptions drawn from phenomenology and especially from Alfred Schutz (1967).

In this approach interviewers use, primarily, open-ended questions. Their major task is to build upon and explore their participants' responses to those questions. The goal is to have the participant reconstruct his or her experience within the topic under study.

The range of topics adaptable to this interviewing approach is wide, covering almost any issue involving the experience of contemporary people. In the past few years, doctoral students with whom I have worked have explored the following subjects in pilot projects, some of which have developed into dissertations and further publications:

Eleventh-grade students as writers (Cleary, 1985, 1988, 1990, in press)
Long-term child care providers

9

African students studying science in the United States
Hispanic teachers teaching in a Hispanic community
Affirmative action officers in higher education
Remedial tutors in an undergraduate math program
ESL teachers (Young, 1990)
Natives of a Spanish-speaking culture teaching in bilingual programs
    in the United States
Teaching students with learning problems stemming from behav-
    ioral issues
"White" antiracism educators
Guidance counselors in a new urban high school
The work of physical education teacher educators (Williamson,
    1988, 1990)
Black jazz musicians who become teachers in colleges and universi-
    ties (Hardin, 1987)
Spanish-speaking teaching assistants who teach Spanish to Anglo-
    American students
Community college students on academic probation
Women returning to community colleges (Schatzkamer, 1986)
Docents in museums
The impact of tracking on student teachers (O'Donnell, 1990)
Lesbian physical education teachers (Woods, 1990)

In each of these pilot and dissertation studies, the interviewer explored
complex issues in the subject area by examining the concrete experience
of people in that area and the meaning their experience had for them.

THE THREE-INTERVIEW SERIES

Perhaps most distinguishing of all its features, this model of in-depth,
phenomenological interviewing involves conducting a series of three separate interviews with each participant. People's behavior becomes meaningful and understandable when placed in the context of their lives and
the lives of those around them. Without context there is little possibility
of exploring the meaning of an experience (Patton, 1989). Interviewers
who propose to explore their topic by arranging a one-shot meeting with
an "interviewee" whom they have never met tread on thin contextual ice
(Mishler, 1986).

Dolbeare and Schuman (Schuman, 1982) designed the series of
three interviews that characterizes this approach and allows the inter-

viewer and participant to plumb the experience and to place it in context. The first interview establishes the context of the participants' experience. The second allows participants to reconstruct the details of their experience within the context in which it occurs. And the third encourages the participants to reflect on the meaning their experience holds for them.

Interview One: Focused Life History

experience in context

In the first interview, the interviewer's task is to put the participant's experience in context by asking him or her to tell as much as possible about him or herself in light of the topic up to the present time. In our study of the experience of student teachers and mentors in a professional development school in East Longmeadow, Massachusetts (O'Donnell et al., 1989), we asked our participants to tell us about their past lives, up until the time they became student teachers or mentors, going as far back as possible within 90 minutes.

We ask them to reconstruct their early experiences in their families, in school, with friends, in their neighborhood, and at work. Because the topic of this interview study is their experience as student teachers or as mentors, we focus on the participants' past experience in school and in any such situations as camp counseling, tutoring, or coaching they might have done before coming to the professional development school program.

In asking them to put their student teaching or mentoring in the context of their life history, we avoid asking "Why did you become a student teacher (or mentor)?" Instead, we ask how they came to be participating in the program. By asking "how?" we hope to have them reconstruct a range of constitutive events in their past family, school, and work experience that place their participation in the professional development school program in the context of their lives.

How? not Why?

Interview Two: The Details of Experience

reconstruct the details

The purpose of the second interview is to concentrate on the concrete details of the participants' present experience in the topic area of the study. We ask them to reconstruct these details. In our study of student teachers and mentors in a clinical site, for example, we ask them what they actually do on the job. We do not ask for opinions but rather the details of their experience, upon which their opinions may be built.

In order to put their experience within the context of the social setting, we ask the student teachers, for example, to talk about their relationships with their students, their mentors, the other faculty in the school, the administrators, the parents, and the wider community. In this second interview, we might ask them to reconstruct a day in their student teaching from the moment they woke up to the time they fell asleep. We ask for stories about their experience in school as a way of eliciting details.

Interview Three: Reflection on the Meaning

In the third interview, participants are asked to reflect on the meaning of their experience. The question of "meaning" is not one of satisfaction or reward, although such issues may play a part in the participants' thinking. Rather, it addresses the intellectual and emotional connections between the participants' work and life. The question might be phrased, "Given what you have said about your life before you became a mentor teacher and given what you have said about your work now, how do you understand mentoring in your life? What sense does it make to you?" This question may take a future orientation; for example, "Given what you have reconstructed in these interviews, where do you see yourself going in the future?"

Making sense or making meaning requires that the participants look at how the factors in their lives interacted to bring them to their present situation. It also requires that they look at their present experience in detail and within the context in which it occurs. The combination of exploring the past to clarify the events that led participants to where they are now, and describing the concrete details of their present experience, establishes conditions for reflecting upon what they are now doing in their lives. The third interview can be productive only if the foundation for it has been established in the first two.

Even though it is in the third interview that we focus on the participants' understanding of their experience, through all three interviews participants are making meaning. The very process of putting experience into language is a meaning-making process (Vygotsky, 1987). When we ask participants to reconstruct details of their experience, they are selecting events from their past and in so doing imparting meaning to them. When we ask participants to tell stories of their experience, they frame some aspect of it with a beginning, a middle, and an end and thereby make it meaningful, whether it is in interview one, two, or three. But in interview three, we focus on that question in the context of the two previous interviews and make that meaning-making the center of our attention.

continuous meaning making

openness   *focus*

RESPECT THE STRUCTURE

We have found it important to adhere to the three-interview structure. Each interview serves a purpose both by itself and within the series. Sometimes, in the first interview, a participant may start to tell an interesting story about his or her present work situation; but that is the focus of the second interview. It is tempting, because the information may be interesting, to pursue the participant's lead and forsake the structure of the interview. To do so, however, can erode the focus of each interview and the interviewer's sense of purpose. Each interview comprises a multitude of decisions that the interviewer must make. The open-ended, in-depth inquiry is best carried out in a structure that allows both the participant and the interviewer to maintain a sense of the focus of each interview in the series.

Furthermore, each interview provides a foundation of detail that helps illumine the next. Taking advantage of the interactive and cumulative nature of the sequence of the interviews requires that interviewers adhere to the purpose of each. There is a logic to the interviews, and to lose control of their direction is to lose the power of that logic and the benefit from it. Therefore, in the process of conducting the three interviews, the interviewer must maintain a delicate balance between providing enough openness for the participants to tell their stories and enough focus to allow the interview structure to work. (See McCracken, 1988, p. 22 for further discussion of this delicate balance.)

LENGTH OF INTERVIEWS

To accomplish the purpose of each of the three interviews, Dolbeare and Schuman (Schuman, 1982) used a 90-minute format. People learning this method for the first time often react, "Oh, that is so long. How will we fill that amount of time? How will we get a participant to agree to be interviewed for that length of time?"

An hour carries with it the consciousness of a standard unit of time that can have participants "watching the clock." Two hours seems too long to sit at one time. Given that the purpose of this approach is to have the participants reconstruct their experience, put it in the context of their lives, and reflect on its meaning, anything shorter than 90 minutes for each interview seems too short. There is, however, nothing magical or absolute about this time frame. For younger participants, a shorter period may be appropriate. What is important is that the length of time be decided upon before the interview process begins.

90 - minutes

Doing so gives unity to each interview; the interview has at least a chronological beginning, middle, and end. Interviewers can learn to hone their skills if they work within a set amount of time and have to fit their technique to it. Furthermore, if interviewers are dealing with a considerable number of participants, they need to schedule their interviews so that they can finish one and go on to the next. As they begin to work with the vast amount of material that is generated in in-depth interviews, they will appreciate having allotted a limited amount of time to each.

The participants have a stake in a set amount of time also. They must know how much time is being asked of them; they have to schedule their lives. Moreover, an open-ended time period can produce undue anxiety. Most participants with whom I have worked come very quickly to appreciate the 90-minute period. Rather than seeming too long, it's long enough to make them feel they are being taken seriously.

At times it is tempting to keep going at the end of the 90 minutes, because what is being discussed at that point is of considerable interest. Although one might gain new insights by continuing the interview beyond the allotted time, it is my experience that a situation of diminishing returns sets in. Extending the interview causes an unraveling of the interviewer's purpose and of the participant's confidence that the interviewer will do what he or she promised.

A related phenomenon is that sometimes participants continue to talk after the interview is concluded and the tape is turned off. It is tempting to continue, because the participants seem suddenly willing to discuss matters heretofore avoided. The problem is that such after-the-fact conversations are not recorded and are not normally covered in the written consent form. (See Chapter 5.) Although the material may seem interesting, it is ultimately difficult to use.

SPACING OF INTERVIEWS

The three-interview structure works best, in my experience, when the researcher can space each interview from 3 days to a week apart. This allows time for the participant to mull over the preceding interview but not enough time to lose the connection between the two. In addition, the spacing allows interviewers to work with the participants over a 2- to 3-week period. This passage of time reduces the impact of possibly idiosyncratic interviews. That is, the participant might be having a terrible day, be sick, or be distracted in such a way as to affect the quality of a particular interview.

In addition, the fact that interviewers come back to talk three times for an hour and a half affects the development of the relationship between the participants and the interviewers positively. The interviewers are asking a lot of the participants; but the interviewers reciprocate with their time and effort. With the contact visits, the telephone calls and letters to confirm schedules and appointments (see Chapter 4), and the three actual interviews, interviewers have an opportunity to establish a substantial relationship with participants over time.

ALTERNATIVES TO THE STRUCTURE AND PROCESS

Researchers will have reasons for exploring alternatives to the structure and procedures described above. As long as a structure is maintained that allows participants to reconstruct their experience within the context of their lives, alterations to the three-interview structure and the duration and spacing of interviews can certainly be explored.

Our research teams have tried variations in spacing, usually necessitated by the schedules of our participants. On occasion, when a participant missed an interview because of an unanticipated complication, we conducted interviews one and two during the same afternoon rather than spacing them a few days or a week apart. And sometimes participants have been unavailable for 2 or 3 weeks. Once a participant said he was leaving for summer vacation the day after we contacted him. We conducted interviews one, two, and three with him all on the same day with reasonable results.

As yet there are no absolutes in the world of interviewing. Relatively little research has been done on the effects of following one procedure over others; most extant research has conceived of interviewing in a stimulus-response frame of reference, which is inadequate to the in-depth procedure (Brenner, Brown, & Canter, 1985; Hyman, Cobb, Fledman, Hart, & Stember, 1954; Kahn & Cannell, 1960; Mishler, 1986; Richardson et al., 1965). The governing principle in designing interviewing might well be to strive for a rational process that is both repeatable and documentable. Remember that it is not a perfect world. It is almost always better to conduct an interview under less than ideal conditions than not to conduct one at all.

WHOSE MEANING IS IT? VALIDITY AND RELIABILITY

Whose meaning is it that an interview brings forth and that a researcher reports in a presentation, article, or book? That is not a simple question. Every aspect of the structure, process, and practice of interviewing can be directed toward the goal of minimizing the effect the interviewer and the interviewing situation have on how the participants reconstruct their experience. No matter how diligently we work to that effect, however, the fact is that interviewers are a part of the interviewing picture. They ask questions, respond to the participant, and at times even share their own experiences. Moreover, interviewers work with the material, select from it, interpret, describe, and analyze it. Though they may be disciplined and dedicated to keeping the interviews as the participants' meaning-making process, interviewers are also a part of that process (Ferrarotti, 1981; Mishler, 1986).

The interaction between the data gatherers and the participants is inherent in the nature of interviewing. It is inherent as well in other qualitative approaches, such as participant observation. And I believe it is also inherent in most experimental and quasi-experimental methodologies applied to human beings, despite the myriad and sophisticated measures developed to control for it (Campbell & Stanley, 1963).

One major difference, however, between qualitative and quantitative approaches is that in in-depth interviewing we recognize and affirm the role of the instrument, the human interviewer. Rather than decrying the fact that the instrument used to gather data affects this process, we say the human interviewer can be a marvelously smart, adaptable, flexible instrument who can respond to situations with skill, tact, and understanding (Lincoln & Guba, 1985, p. 107).

Although the interviewer can strive to have the meaning being made in the interview as much a function of the participant's reconstruction and reflection as possible, the interviewer must nevertheless recognize that the meaning is, to some degree, a function of the participant's interaction with the interviewer. Only by recognizing that interaction and affirming its possibilities can interviewers use their skills (see Chapter 6) to minimize the distortion (see Patton, 1989, p. 157) that can occur because of their role in the interview.

Is It Anybody's Meaning?

How do we know that what the participant is telling us is true? And if it is true for this participant, is it true for anyone else? And if another person were doing the interview, would we get a different meaning? Or if we were to do the interview at a different time of year, would the participant reconstruct his or her experience differently? Or if we had picked different participants to interview, would we get an entirely dissimilar and perhaps contradictory sense of the issue at hand? These are some of the questions underlying the issues of validity, reliability, and generalizability that researchers confront.

Many qualitative researchers disagree with the epistemological assumptions underlying the notion of validity. They argue for a new vocabulary and rhetoric with which to discuss validity and reliability (Mishler, 1986, pp. 108–110). Lincoln and Guba (1985), for example, substitute the notion of "trustworthiness" for that of validity. In a careful exposition they argue that qualitative researchers must inform what they do by concepts of "credibility," "transferability," "dependability," and "confirmability" (pp. 289–332).

Others criticize the idea of objectivity that underlies notions of reliability and validity. Ferrarotti (1981) argues that the most profound knowledge can be gained only by the deepest intersubjectivity among researchers and that which they are researching. Such a discussion suggests that neither the vocabulary of "validity" nor "trustworthiness" is adequate.

Yet, in-depth interviewers can respond to the question, "Are the participant's comments valid?" The three-interview structure incorporates features that enhance the accomplishment of validity. It places participants' comments in context. It encourages interviewing participants over the course of 1 to 3 weeks to account for idiosyncratic days and to check for the internal consistency of what they say. Furthermore, by interviewing a number of participants, we can connect their experiences and check the comments of one participant against those of others. Finally, the goal of the process is to understand how our participants understand and make meaning of their experience. If the interview structure works to allow them to make sense to themselves as well as to the interviewer, then it has gone a long way toward validity.

An Example of an Approach to Validity

One participant in our Secondary Teacher Education Program was a woman who had taught in parochial schools for a number of years but was not certified. She had enrolled in our program to get certified at the high school level in social studies. She agreed to be interviewed about her experience in our clinical site teacher education program.

The interviewer began her third interview with its basic question: "What does it mean to you to be a student teacher?" She responded:

> Well, I guess—well, . . . [small laugh]—it kinda—it really kind of means that I've finally gotten down to actually trying to—I guess what it means is—[it] is the final passage into making a commitment to this, the profession, to teaching as—as a profession. What am I going to do with my life because I have all—all this time, going up and down and in and out of

teaching. Should I or shouldn't I? I was kind of stuck in that space where people say, you know, "Oh, those who can't, teach. Those who can, do." Just the whole negative status that teaching and education have. So it's kind of fraught with that. And really resisting the fact that I had to student teach. I mean, I can remember [that] holding me back, what, 10 years ago, thinking, "Oh, no, I will actually have to be a student teacher some day," and remembered what student teachers were like in my high school, and thinking "Oh, I'll never humiliate myself that way." [small laugh] And so I guess it was the final — [pause] — biting the bullet to . . . making a commitment.

Is what she says valid? In the first interview she recounted how she had dropped out of college and taught in elementary grades in parochial schools because she needed money. In that interview she also talked about how she had dropped out of education courses because she didn't think she was getting enough out of them; how she had switched to an academic field, but later realized that she really liked teaching.

The material in her third interview is internally consistent with the material in her first, which was given 2 weeks earlier. Internal consistency over a period of time leads one to trust that she is not lying to the interviewer. Furthermore, there is enough in the syntax, the pauses, the groping for words, the self-effacing laughter, to make a reader believe that she is grappling seriously with the question of what student teaching means to her, and that what she is saying is true for her at the time she is saying it.

Moreover, in reading the transcript, we see that the interviewer has kept quiet, not interrupted her, not tried to redirect her thinking while she was developing it; so her thoughts seem to be hers and not the interviewer's. These are her words and they reflect her understanding of her experience at the time of her interview.

When I read this passage, I learned something both about this particular student and about an aspect of the student-teaching experience that had not really been apparent to me. I began to think about aspects of the process we require prior to student teaching that enhance the need for students to make a commitment and about other aspects of our program that minimize that need. I began to wonder what the conditions are that encourage a person to make that commitment.

Finally, what the participant said about the status of education as a career and how that related to her personal indecision is consistent with what we know the literature says about the teaching profession and with what other participants in our study have said. I can relate this individual passage to a broader discourse on the issue.

The interview allowed me to get closer to understanding this student teacher's experience than I would have been able to do by other methods such as questionnaires or observation. I cannot say that her understanding of student teaching as a commitment is valid for others, although passages in other interviews connect to what she has said. I can say that it seems valid for her at this point in her life. I cannot say that her understanding of the meaningfulness of student teaching as a commitment she had heretofore not been willing to make will not change. Unlike the laws of physics, there is nothing unchanging about human life and social interaction except that we die. There is no solid, unmovable platform upon which to base our understanding of human affairs. They are in constant flux. Heisenberg's principle of indeterminacy (Lincoln & Guba, 1985; Polanyi, 1958) speaks at least as directly to human affairs as it does to the world of physics.

The structure of the three interviews, the passage of time over which the interviews occur, the internal consistency and possible external consistency of the passages, the syntax, diction, and even nonverbal aspects of the passage, and the discovery and sense of learning that I get from reading the passage lead me to have confidence in its authenticity. Because we are concerned with the participant's understanding of her experience, the authenticity of what she is saying makes it reasonable for me to have confidence in its validity for her.

Avoiding a Mechanistic Response

There is room in the universe for multiple approaches to validity. The problem is not in the multiplicity. Rather it lies in the sometimes doctrinaire ways some advocates of divergent approaches polarize the issue. (See Gage, 1989.) Those who advocate qualitative approaches are in danger of becoming as doctrinaire as those who once held the monopoly on educational research and advocated quantitative approaches.

On occasion I see dissertations in which doctoral candidates are as mechanical about establishing an "audit trail" or devising methods of "triangularization" (Lincoln & Guba, 1985, p. 283) as those in my generation who dutifully devised procedures to confront "instrument decay" and "experimental mortality" (Campbell & Stanley, 1966, p. 79, 182). What are needed are not formulaic approaches to enhancing either validity or trustworthiness but understanding of and respect for the issues that underlie those terms. We must grapple with them, doing our best to increase our ways of knowing and of avoiding ignorance, realizing that our efforts are quite small in the larger scale of things.

EXPERIENCE THE PROCESS YOURSELF

Before readers go much further with this approach to interviewing, I recommend that they test their interest in it and explore some of the issues by doing a practice project. Team up with a peer. Interview each other about your experience in your present job or as a graduate student. (If you are doing this practice project as part of a class, this exercise can lead to some significant understanding about what graduate study is like in your school.)

Use the three-interview structure. Since this is practice to become acquainted with the technique, shorten, if you choose to do so, the time normally allotted to each interview from 90 minutes to 30 minutes. In the first interview, ask your peer participant about how she came to her work or her graduate study. Find out as much as possible about the context of her life leading up to her present position or to her status as a graduate student.

In the second interview, ask your participant to tell you as much as possible about the details of her job experience or her work as a graduate student. Ask, "What is your work? What is it like for you to do what you do?"

In the third interview, ask your participant what her work or her experience as a graduate student means to her. You might say, "Now that you have talked about how you came to your work (or to be a graduate student), and what it is like for you to do that work (or be a student), what does it mean to you?"

Arrange appointments for each of the interviews. Tape record them, and be sure to arrange to be interviewed by your peer participant in return.

The point of this practice project is to experience interviewing and being interviewed and to see whether you connect to the possibilities of the process. The practice project should alert you to how the way you are as a person affects your interviewing. You may notice how difficult it is for you to stay quiet and let another person speak while at the same time being an active listener and following up on what your participant has said. You may become aware of issues of control and focus. You may find that you have little patience for or interest in other people's stories; or you may connect to their possibilities.

3

Proposing Research:
From Mind to Paper to Action

Research proposal writing is substantively and symbolically an important event. In an excellent book on the subject, *Proposals That Work*, Locke, Spirduso, and Silverman (1987) say that a dissertation proposal has three substantive functions: to plan, to communicate, and to establish a contract. There is, however, a fourth function. Developing a dissertation proposal and getting it approved is a crucial step in the rite of passage of earning a doctorate. Its ritualistic function can sometimes make writing a proposal seem daunting. It transforms the writer of the proposal from the status of student to that of researcher.

RESEARCH PROPOSALS AS RITES OF PASSAGE

In some respects becoming an academic is like joining a club. As in most other somewhat exclusive clubs, there are those who are in and those who are out; there are elites and non-elites. There are privileges of membership and there are penalties for not paying dues. To some extent, success in the club is a matter of merit; but that success is sometimes affected by issues of race, gender, and class that can influence entry into the club in the first place, or weight the power of those who have been admitted already.

Although there are pressures, strains, and contradictions in working in collegiate institutions just as there are in others, still college faculty are paid for the pleasurable work of reading, writing, teaching, and doing research. Relative to public school teachers, for example, we have a great deal of autonomy over our time and professional lives. Not all doctoral candidates in education move on to faculty positions in colleges or universities. But those who use their doctorates to assume leadership positions in school systems also often gain a degree of autonomy in their working lives that many would envy.

Those who have already earned the doctorate often act as gatekeepers to the club. During the rituals of proposal submission, review, and approval established by the gatekeepers, the power relationship between candidate and doctoral advisor is very unequal. Elements of sexism, racism, classism, and institutional politics can enter the process. When that relationship is inequitable, the rite of passage can be excessively anxiety producing. It takes a great deal of thoughtfulness on everyone's part to make the relationship between doctoral candidate and committee equitable at the proposal stage.

COMMITMENT

When a candidate's doctoral program is working well, a research topic arises out of work that has gone before. Course work, fieldwork, practica, clinical work, and comprehensive exams all lead the candidate forward to an area of inquiry about which he or she feels some passion. If the doctoral program has not worked well — if committee memberships have changed, if the doctoral student has been convinced against his or her own interests to pursue those of a professor — a student can progress through the earlier stages of the rite of passage without identifying a topic that is personally meaningful. In that case, predictably the writing of the proposal will be more excruciating than satisfying.

In some cases doctoral candidates enter the program having already chosen a topic. For a while they make their peers nervous because they seem so advanced and confident. My sense is that such confidence is often misplaced. The experience of the doctoral program itself should bring about some sort of new orientation, some interest in new areas, some growth in the candidate's outlook. If it does not, the candidate is looking backward instead of forward.

Substantively, one of the underlying reasons for writing a proposal is its planning function (Locke et al., 1987). To plan, candidates must assess where they have been and make a commitment to where they would like to go. This can be a stressful part of the process.

I remember one outstanding doctoral candidate who was stalled for 6 months at the prospect of writing his dissertation proposal. It was not that he could not find a subject; nor was he in search of a method. He was just frozen in his writing. After 6 months of not being able to get around his writing block, he finally discussed his anxieties about, in effect, changing club memberships. He said that he had grown up in a working-class neighborhood where people sat on their front-porch steps in the summer drinking beer. That was what his parents still did. He was not sure that he wanted to leave the front porch to start drinking white wine in the living room at faculty gatherings. For many doctoral candidates, completing their dissertations implies a commitment to a new professional and personal identity that can be difficult to make.

FROM THOUGHT TO LANGUAGE

Students also have trouble writing proposals because they are plagued by a sense of audience. The process seems dominated by doctoral committees, and sometimes a more anonymous graduate review committee, that must approve the proposal. When audience plays such a dominating role, writing can easily suffer. Rather than concentrating on what he or she wants to say, the candidate may filter every sentence through the screen of what is expected and what will be acceptable to the committee.

Preliminary ideas about research often stay locked in one's inner speech. They are fleeting, predicated, and unstable (Vygotsky, 1987), making communication of them difficult. However, those ideas in inner speech must be made explicit. Doctoral candidates do have to communicate clearly to their committee what they are thinking about.

A key to communicating about plans for research is to focus first on what is meaningful. When a proposal works best, it emanates from the motives of the candidate and works its way through thought, inner speech, and into external speech through meaning. Often, however, the form and substance of the inquiry in a dissertation proposal can seem to the candidate to be imposed from the outside; the format of dissertation proposals can seem to take precedence over their substance. Then the writing of the proposal can become mechanical and formulaic.

WHAT IS TO BE DONE?

Peter Elbow (1981) offers an approach to writing that I think can be useful in such cases. He suggests that trying both to create with the audience in mind and to make writing perfect from the start imposes an undue burden on the writing process. He suggests making writing and editing two separate aspects of the writing process. And he urges deferring thoughts of the audience until the editing part of the process.

To facilitate that separation, Elbow suggests what has come to be

known as free-writing and focused free-writing. Focused free-writing is
a process that allows the writer to concentrate on the topic and forget
the audience. It advises writers to start writing on their topics and to
continue for a specified period of time without stopping. If they get stuck,
they should repeat their last word or write the word *stuck* until they get
going again. A person new to the process might begin with 5 minutes of
focused free-writing, gradually increasing the length of time.

After free-writing sections of the proposal, writers can then select
from these the most cogent, refashioning from them a first draft. Elbow
suggests other methods to help writers overcome blocks due to anxiety
about audience. Near the end of the writing process, rather than at the
beginning, writers can edit their drafts with the audience and the form of
dissertation proposal in mind. I recommend both Elbow's (1981) *Writing
With Power* and Locke, Spirduso, and Silverman's (1987) *Proposals That
Work* as important resources for anyone about to write a dissertation
proposal.

QUESTIONS TO STRUCTURE THE PROPOSAL

What?

Proposal writers need to ask themselves some simple questions. These
can be divided into several groups. First is a group of questions I put
under the heading of "What?" In what am I interested? What am I trying
to learn about and understand? What is the basis of my interest?

Interviewers begin with an interest in a particular area. At the beginning of interviewers' research lurks the desire to understand what is going
on. But how did that desire begin? Important questions that must be
asked in interviewing research and that are seldom asked in experimental
or quasi-experimental research are, What is the context of my interest?
How did I come to this interest? What are the factors in my experience
that led me to become interested in this area of inquiry? What is my stake
in the inquiry? How did I become interested in it, and what do I get out
of pursuing my interest and learning about it? What are my expectations
about the subject of inquiry?

Research, like almost everything else in life, has autobiographical
roots. It is crucial for interviewers to identify the autobiographical roots
of their interest in their topic. Research is hard work; interviewing research is especially so. In order to sustain the energy needed to do the
research well, a researcher must have some passion about his or her
subject. Rather than seeking a "disinterested" position as a researcher,

the interviewer needs to understand and affirm his or her interest in order to build on the energy that can come from it. Equally important, researchers must identify the source of their interest in order to channel it appropriately. They must acknowledge it in order to minimize the distortion such interest can cause in the way they carry out their interviewing. An autobiographical section explaining researchers' connections to their proposed research seems to me to be crucial for those interested in in-depth interviewing.

Finally, interviewers must not only identify their connection with the subject of the interview; they must also affirm that their interest in the subject reflects a real desire to know what is going on, to understand the experience. If in fact interviewers are so intimately connected to the subject of inquiry that they really do not feel perplexed, and what they are really hoping to do is corroborate their own experience, they will not have enough distance from the subject to interview effectively. The questions will not be real; that is, they will not be questions to which the interviewers do not already have the answers.

Why? in Context

The next question to ask is why the subject might be important to others. Why is the subject significant? What is the background of this subject and why is that background important to understand? To what else does the subject relate? If you understand the complexities of this subject, what will be the benefit and who will obtain it? What is the context of previous work that has been done on the subject (Locke et al., 1987)? How will your work build on what has been done already?

Locke and his colleagues are especially cogent in their discussion of what often appears in dissertation proposals as "reviews of the literature." They stress that these sometimes mechanical summaries of previous research miss the intent of reading the literature connected to the subject. Such reading should inform researchers of the context of the research, allow them to gain a better sense of the issue's significance and how it has been approached before, as well as reveal what is missing in the previous research. These understandings can be integrated into the various sections of the proposal and do not necessitate a separate one that sometimes reads like a book report. (See Locke et al., 1987, chap. 3.)

In addition to asking why the topic is historically significant, critical ethnographers suggest that how the topic relates to issues of power, justice, and oppression must also be raised. Especially important are the issues of power that are implicit in the research topic itself (Solsken, 1989) and in interviewing as a methodology. John Rowan (1981) suggests that researchers consider not only how their own personal interests are served by their research but also who else's interest is served. What about the participants in the research? What do they get out of participating? What do they risk? Does the research underwrite any existing patterns of oppression? Or does the research offer some possibility of understanding that could create liberating energy? In a world beset by inequity, why is the topic of research important? (See Fay, 1987, for an important discussion of the foundations of critical social science.)

How?

A next question to ask is, How? Assuming that researchers have decided that in-depth interviewing is appropriate for their study, how can they adapt the structure of in-depth, phenomenological interviewing outlined in Chapter 2 to their subject of study?

To offer one example, Marguerite Sheehan (1989), a doctoral candidate in early childhood education at the University of Massachusetts, addressed the question as follows. She was interested in studying child care as a career. In her review of the literature she had found that most of the research on child-care providers focused on those who had left the field early because of what was called "burn-out." Sheehan was interested in people who stayed in the field, especially those who saw providing child care as a career. She hoped to come to understand the nature of their experience and to see if she could unravel some of the factors that contributed to their longevity in the field. Sheehan took the three-interview structure and adapted it as follows:

Interview One (life history): How did the participant come to be a child-care provider? A review of the participant's life history up to the time he or she became a child-care provider.

Interview Two (contemporary experience): What is it like for the participant to be a child-care provider? What are the details of the participant's work as a child-care provider?

Interview Three: What does it mean to the participant to be a child-care provider? Given what the participant has said in interviews one and two, how does he or she make sense of his or her work as a child-care provider?

Who? When? Where?

The next set of questions asks whom the researchers will interview, and how they will get access and make contact with their participants. In Chapter 4 we discuss the complexities of access, contact, and selecting participants. What is called for at this point is a consideration of the strategy the researchers will use. What will the range of participants be? What strategy of gaining access to them will the researchers use? How will they make contact with them? The strategy may allow for a process of participant selection that evolves over the course of the study, but the structure and strategy for that selection must be thought out in the proposal.

Some writers suggest that the "how" of a qualitative research study can itself be emergent as the study proceeds. That orientation assumes that because qualitative research does not begin with a set of hypotheses to test, strict control of variables is not necessary. Furthermore, because the inquiry is being done in order to learn about complexities of which researchers are not totally aware, the design and even the focus of the study have to be seen as "emergent" (Lincoln & Guba, 1985, pp. 208–211, pp. 224–225).

Although it is understandable that researchers would want to build flexibility into a research design, there is a danger in overemphasizing the "emergent" nature of research design in qualitative research. To the inexperienced, it can appear to minimize the need for careful preparation and planning. It can lead to the notion that qualitative research is somehow an "art" that really is incommunicable, or that somehow those who engage in it have earned a special status because they do not share the assumptions of those who do what is called quantitative research (McCracken, 1988, pp. 12–13). The danger of overemphasizing the "emergent" nature of the design of the study is a looseness, lack of focus, and misplaced nonchalance about purpose, method, and procedure on the part of those who do qualitative research. Lincoln and Guba (1985) themselves stress that the emergent nature of qualitative research cannot be used as a license for "undisciplined and haphazard 'poking around'" (p. 251).

RATIONALE

Although the paradigms that underlie research methods in the social sciences seem to be changing rapidly (Lincoln & Guba, 1985), the extent to which researchers will have to defend their use of in-depth interviewing as their research methodology will depend on their individual departments. Some are still dominated by experimentalism or other forms of quantitative research. In others there may be a predisposition to experimental and quasi-experimental methods but nevertheless an openness to qualitative research. In still others there may be a strong preference for qualitative research among a significant number of the faculty.

Whatever the departmental context, for the interviewing process to be meaningful to researchers themselves and its use credible to reviewers, it is important that researchers understand why they are choosing interviewing rather than experimental or quasi-experimental research. They must understand something about the history of science, the development of positivism, and the critique of positivism as it is applied to the social sciences in general and the field of education in particular.

Because there is currently more acceptance of qualitative research in graduate programs in education, many new researchers have not been asked to learn the assumptions and the practices of experimental or quasi-experimental research. Without this background, qualitative researchers do not know what they do not know about methodology. Consequently, their rationale for choosing a qualitative over a quantitative approach may not be as well grounded as it could be.

At the minimum, Campbell and Stanley's (1963) definitive essay on threats to what they call internal and external validity in experimental and quasi-experimental research should be required reading for all those who intend to do interviewing and other forms of qualitative research. They should grapple firsthand with the issues that shaped a generation of educational researchers and that still inform a significant body of educational research practice today. Even better would be thoughtful reading in the history of science and epistemology. (See, e.g., James, 1947; Johnson, 1975; Lincoln & Guba, 1985; Matson, 1966; Mannheim, 1975; Polanyi, 1958.)

WORKING WITH THE MATERIAL

Research proposals should describe how researchers intend to work with, analyze, describe, and share the material they gather. Describing this process ahead of time is especially difficult for those who are doing empirical research for the first time. It is difficult to project how they will work with material from interview participants if they have never done interviewing work before. In Chapter 8, I discuss working with the material. I stress the importance of paying attention to the words of the participant, using those words to report on the results as much as possible, and looking for both salient material within individual interviews and connections among interviews and participants.

The role that theory plays becomes an issue when researchers are actually trying to analyze and interpret the material they gather. Some scholars would argue that the theory used to discern and forge relationships among the words that participants share with interviewers must come out of those words themselves. Theory cannot and should not be imposed on the words but must emanate from them. This approach, extensively discussed by Glaser and Strauss (1967), has been persuasive in the field of qualitative research. It argues, rightly I think, especially against taking theoretical frameworks developed in other contexts and force-fitting the words of the participants into the matrices developed from those theories.

On the other hand, it may be naive for us to argue that researchers can be theory free. Everyone has theories. They are the explanations people develop to help them make connections among events. Theories are not the private preserve of scientists. Interviewers walk into interviews with theories about human behavior, teaching and learning, the organization of schools, and the way societies work. Some of their theories are informed and supported by others, and some are very idiosyncratic. Others arise from readings interviewers have done in and about the subject of their inquiry.

Some scholars argue that in qualitative research such reading should be kept to a minimum lest it contaminate the view and the understanding of the researcher (Glaser & Strauss, 1967). To a certain extent, I agree with that view. It helps to interview participants about their experience if the interviewers are not weighted down with preformed ideas based on what they have gleaned from the literature. No reading is likely to match the individual stories of participants' experience, but reading can help make those stories more understandable by providing a context for them.

The range of fields and associated readings that those who do research in education must synthesize is daunting. Often, we fall short of the task. But for those who take the task seriously, it is first-rate intellectual work. This work should be affirmed and represented in the proposal.

PILOTING YOUR WORK

The best advice I ever received as a researcher was to do a pilot of my proposed study. The dictionary (Gove, 1971) definition of the verb *pilot* is "to guide along strange paths or through dangerous places" (p. 1716). Although it may not seem ahead of time that the world of interviewing research takes one along strange paths or through dangerous places, the unanticipated twists and turns of the interviewing process and the complexities of the interviewing relationship deserve exploration before the researchers plunge headlong into the thick of their projects.

I urge all interviewing researchers to build into their proposal a pilot venture in which they try out their interviewing design with a small number of participants. They will learn whether their research structure is appropriate for the study they envision. They will come to grips with some of the practical aspects of establishing access, making contact, and conducting the interview. The pilot can alert them to elements of their own interview techniques that support the objectives of the study and to those that detract from those objectives. After completing the pilot, researchers can step back, reflect on their experience, discuss it with their doctoral committee, and revise their research approach based on what they have learned from their pilot experience. (See Locke et al., 1987, pp. 66–69 for a more extensive discussion of pilot studies.)

CONCLUSION

As teachers must plan their objectives and how their methods fit those objectives in order to be responsive to what they meet in their classrooms, so too must researchers plan carefully for research. They must be thoughtful about the what, why, how, who, when, and where of interviewing. They must be as focused and clear as possible about their inquiry when they begin the study. Such planning is the prerequisite for being able to respond thoughtfully and carefully to what emerges as the study proceeds.

Because in-depth interviewing uses a method that is essentially open-ended, preparation, planning, and structure are crucial. Each interview requires a series of instantaneous decisions about what direction to take. Researchers entering an interviewing situation without a plan, sense of purpose, or structure within which to carry out that purpose have little on which to base those decisions. Without a thoughtful structure for their work, they increase the chance of distorting what they learn from their participants (Hyman et al., 1954) and of imposing their own sense of the world on their participants rather than eliciting theirs.

4

Establishing Access To, Making Contact With, and Selecting Participants

Before selecting participants for an interview study, the interviewer must both establish access to them and make contact. Because interviewing involves a relationship between the interviewer and the participant, how interviewers gain access to potential participants and make contact with them can affect the beginning of that relationship and every subsequent step in the interviewing process. In this and subsequent chapters, I discuss an idea that I think is equivalent to the First Commandment of interviewing: Be equitable. Respect the participant and yourself. In developing the interviewing relationship, consider what is fair and just to the participant and to you.

THE PERILS OF EASY ACCESS

Beginning interviewers, like running water, tend to look for the easiest path to the goal, their potential participants. They often want to select people with whom they already have a relationship: friends, those with whom they work, students they teach, or others with whom they have some tangential connection. This is understandable but problematic. My experience is that the easier the access, the more complicated the interview.

Interviewing People Whom You Supervise

Conflicts of interest are inherent in interviewing people you supervise. For example, I worked with a doctoral candidate who was the principal of an elementary school. She wanted to interview teachers in her school about their experience in developing collaborative learning projects in their classrooms. She had been deeply involved in the project with her teachers and was eager to understand what effect it had had on their experiences.

In discussions with me the principal said that her school was small and not a large, unfeeling bureaucracy. She had a close working relationship with the teachers. She felt that they trusted her. Finally, she thought that despite her investment in the project, she could be impartial in the interview.

One of the principles of an equitable interviewing relationship, however, is that the participants not make themselves unduly vulnerable by participating in the interview. In any hierarchical school system, no matter how small, in which a principal has hiring and firing power and control over other working conditions, a teacher being interviewed by the principal may not feel free to talk openly. That is especially the case when the teachers know that the interviewer has an investment in the program. The issue in such cases is not whether the principal can achieve enough distance from the subject to allow her to explore fully, but rather whether the teachers feel secure in that exploration. If they do not, the outcomes of such interviews are not likely to be productive.

As a general principle then, it is wise to avoid interviewing participants whom you supervise. That does not mean in this case that the doctoral candidate could not explore the experiences of elementary teachers in collaborative learning projects; it does mean that she had to seek to understand the experience of teachers in schools other than her own.

Interviewing Your Students

Inexperienced interviewers who are also teachers often conceptualize a study that involves interviewing students, and they are often sorely tempted to interview their own. As legitimate as it may be to want to understand the effectiveness of, say, a teaching method or a curriculum, a student can hardly be open to his or her teacher who has both so much power and so much invested in the situation. The teacher-researcher should seek to interview students in some other setting with some other teacher who is using a similar method or curriculum.

Interviewing Acquaintances

Sometimes new interviewers want to select participants whom they know but not in a way related to the subject of study. For example, one doctoral candidate was contemplating an interview study about the complexities of being a cooperating teacher for social studies student teachers. He wanted to interview a participant with whom he did not work professionally but with whom he had regular contact at church. Even experienced interviewers cannot anticipate some of the uncomfortable situations that may develop in an interview. Having to consider not only the interviewing relationship but a church relationship as well might limit the full potential of such an interview.

For example, in an interview about the experience of being a cooperating teacher, the acquaintance from church might reveal that the reason he or she takes on student teachers is for the free time it allows. Normally, an interviewer would want to follow up on an aspect of an interview that made him or her feel uneasy, but to do so in this case could affect his relationship with the participant at church. The interviewer may avoid a follow-up, slant the follow-up, or in some other way distort the interview process because of concern for his or her other relationship with the participant. The result is either incomplete or distorted information on a key aspect of the subject of study.

Interviewing Friends

Some new interviewers with whom I have worked want to interview participants to whom they have easy access because of friendship. The interviewing relationship in such cases can seldom develop on its own merit. It is affected by the friendship in obvious and less obvious ways.

One of the less obvious is that the interviewers and the participants who are friends usually assume that they understand each other. Instead of exploring assumptions and seeking clarity about events and experiences, they tend to assume that they know what is being said. The interviewer and the participant need to have enough distance from each other that they take nothing for granted (see Bogdan & Taylor, 1975; Hyman et al., 1954; McCracken, 1988; Spradley, 1979).

Taking Oneself Just Seriously Enough

In addition to feeling shy about a process with which they have had little practice (Hyman et al., 1954), a major reason that some doctoral candidates with whom I have worked want to capitalize on easy access is that they tend not to take themselves seriously as researchers. Beginning interviewers find it difficult to imagine asking strangers to spend 4½ hours with them.

Many doctoral candidates see research as something others do. Our educational system is structured so that most people consume research but seldom produce it. This has led many to adopt an uncritical attitude about published material and to regard it as somehow sacred. Doing research is seen as an elite occupation, done only by those at the top of the hierarchy (see Bernstein, 1975).

At the same time, when dissertation research does not grow organically out of the course work, clinical experiences, and independent reading that have gone before, it becomes a requirement to be overcome. Doctoral candidates who have had little practice in doing research and who see it as a hurdle rather than an opportunity find it difficult to affirm their own interest in their subject, their own status as researchers, the power of their research method, or the utility of their work other than to fulfill a requirement.

Cumulative societal inequities can exact a heavy toll on researchers at this juncture. Research in our society has long been seen as a male preserve, especially a white male preserve, associated with class and privilege. New researchers who are not middle-class, white males may have to struggle against social conventions to take themselves seriously in their task. Some doctoral candidates need bracing from their advisors and their peers at this point in their program in order to affirm themselves as researchers. Taking oneself seriously enough as a researcher is a first step toward establishing equity in the interviewing relationship.

ACCESS THROUGH FORMAL GATEKEEPERS

When interviewers try to contact potential participants whom they do not know, they often face gatekeepers who control access to those peoples. Gatekeepers can range from absolutely legitimate (to be respected) to self-declared (to be avoided). If a researcher's study involves participants below the age of 18, for example, access to them must involve the absolutely legitimate gatekeepers, their parents or guardians. Although it may be appropriate to seek access to students through the schools, very soon in the process that access must be affirmed by the parents of the children. Within the schools themselves, teachers, principals, and superintendents serve as gatekeepers who must be respected.

Some participants are accessible only through the institutions in which they reside or work. For example, if a researcher wanted to interview prisoners about prison education programs, it is not likely that there would be any route of access other than through the warden. A researcher studying the experience of people at a particular site, whether it be factory, school, church, human service organization, or business, must gain access through the person who has responsibility for the operation of the site. (See Lincoln & Guba, 1985, p. 252; Richardson et al., 1965, p. 97.)

On the other hand, one researching an experience or a process that takes place in a number of sites, but not studying the workings of any purticulur citu, muy not nuud to suvk aoouss through an authority. Such a researcher may want to study the work of high school teachers who teach in many schools scattered through a region. In such a case, the researcher can go directly to them without asking for permission from their principals.

Likewise, a researcher studying the experience of students in high school, but not in a particular high school, might not have to seek access through a principal but only through parents. In general, the more adult the potential participants, the more likely that access can be direct.

In our study of community college faculty (Seidman, 1985) my colleagues and I interviewed 76 participants in approximately 25 different community colleges in Massachusetts, New York State, and California. Because we were not studying a particular community college, we did not seek access to individual faculty through the administrators of the colleges. On the other hand, we were never secretive about our work; it would have been difficult to be so, carrying, as we were, a tape recorder large enough to allow us to make audiotapes of a sound quality suitable for the film that we made in the first phase of our research (Sullivan & Seidman, 1982). But even if we had been using a small, pocket-sized tape recorder, we would not have hidden our research from others. When asked in the halls what we were doing at the college, we answered explicitly about our project.

On only one occasion was a faculty member uncomfortable with our approaching him directly and not through his administration. We told him that he should inform the administration of our project and our wish to interview him; we made it clear that we were not doing research about the site. We said that if an administrator wanted to meet with us, we would be happy to do so in order to explain our project, but we were not eager to seek permission from administrators to interview individual faculty. The participant did inform his administration, but no one wanted to meet us.

INFORMAL GATEKEEPERS

Sometimes although there is no formal gatekeeper, there is an informal one (Richardson et al., 1965). Most faculties, for example, usually include a few members who are widely respected and looked to for guidance when decisions about whether or not to support an effort are made. In small groups, there is usually at least one person who, without having formal authority, nevertheless holds moral suasion. If that person participates in a project, then it must be O.K.; if he or she doesn't, then the group feels there must be a good reason for not doing so. To the extent that interviewers can identify informal gatekeepers, not to use them formally for seeking access to others but to gain their participation in the project as a sign of respect for the effort, access to others in the group may be facilitated.

On the other hand, groups often have self-appointed gatekeepers, who feel they must be informed and must try to control everything that goes on, even if they have no formal authority. Their self-importance is not respected by others in the group; avoiding their involvement in the study may be the best way to facilitate access to others in such a group.

ACCESS AND HIERARCHY

One of the differences between research and evaluation or policy studies is that the latter are often sponsored by an agency close to the people who participate in the interviews. In such studies, authority for access to participants often is formally granted by administrators in charge. There is a sense of official sponsorship of the project (Lincoln & Guba, 1985), which affects the equity of the relationship between interviewer and participant. It is almost as if the interviewer were someone higher in the hierarchy instead of outside it.

Whenever possible, it is important to establish access to participants through their peers rather than through people "above" or "below" them in their hierarchy. For interviewing children, peer access may not be feasible. But in other situations, the demand of equity in the interviewing relationship calls for peer access when possible. If your participants are teachers, for example, try to establish access to them through other teachers; if they are counselors, reach them if at all possible through other counselors.

MAKING CONTACT

Do it yourself. Try not to rely on third parties to make contact with your potential participants. No matter how expedient it seems to have someone else who knows potential participants explain your project to them, try to avoid their doing so. Building the interviewing relationship begins the moment the potential participant hears of the study. Third parties may be very familiar with potential participants, but they can seldom do justice to the nature of someone else's project. They have not internalized it the way the researcher has; they do not have the investment in it that the researcher does. Once having introduced the subject, they can seldom respond to questions that naturally might arise. Third parties may be necessary for gaining access to potential participants but should be used as little as possible to make actual contact with them.

A contact visit before the actual interview aids in selecting participants and helps build a foundation for the interview relationship. A contact visit can also convince an interviewer that a good interviewing relationship with a particular potential participant is not likely to develop. The more care and thoroughness interviewers put into making contact, the better foundation they establish for the interviewing relationship.

MAKE A CONTACT VISIT IN PERSON

Telephoning is often a necessary first step in making contact, but if possible it should consist of only a brief introduction, an explanation of how the interviewer gained access to the person's name, and setting up an appointment to meet. Avoid asking the potential participant for a yes or no answer about participating. An easy "yes" from someone who has not met the interviewer nor heard enough about the interviews can backfire later. A "no" that is a defense against too much initial pressure gets the interviewer nowhere (see Richardson et al., 1967, p. 97). The major purpose of the telephone contact is to set up a time when the interviewer and the potential participant can meet in person to discuss the study.

It takes time, money, and effort to arrange a separate contact visit with individual potential participants or even a group, but they are almost always well spent. The purpose of the contact visit is at least threefold. The most important is to lay the groundwork for the mutual respect necessary to the interview process. By taking the time to make a separate contact visit to introduce him or herself and the study, an interviewer is saying implicitly to the potential participants, "You are important. I take you seriously. I respect my work and you enough to want to make a separate trip to meet with you to explain the project."

Although individual contact visits tend to be more effective, it is possible also to meet with a group of potential participants. Group contact visits save time and wear on the interviewer by allowing one explanation of the study to several people at once. On the downside, one potential participant's skepticism about participating can affect the attitude of others in the group.

Clearly, interviewers will not always be able to make in-person contact and will have to rely on the telephone. In either case, it is important at this point to present the nature of the study in as broad a context as possible and to be explicit about what will be expected of the participant. Seriousness but friendliness of tone, purposefulness but flexibility in approach, and openness but conciseness in presentation are characteristics that can enhance a contact visit whether conducted in person or on the phone. (For discussions of the importance of the first contact, see Dexter, 1970, p. 34; Hyman et al., 1954, p. 201; and Marshall & Rossman, 1989, p. 65.)

The contact visit allows the interviewer to become familiar with the setting in which potential participants live or work before the interview starts. It also allows interviewers to find their way to potential participants so that they are better able to keep their interviewing appointments. In addition to building mutual respect and explaining the nature of the interview study, a second important purpose of the contact visit is to determine whether the potential participant is interested. In-depth interviewing asks a great deal of both participant and interviewer. It is no trivial matter to arrange three 90-minute interviews spaced as much as a week apart. It is important that the potential participant understand the nature of the study, how he or she fits into it, and the purpose of the three-interview sequence.

The contact visit also initiates the process of informed consent, which is necessary in some and desirable in almost all interviewing research. (See Chapter 5.) Although I seldom show the informed consent form in the contact visit, I go over orally all aspects of the study that the consent form usually covers, so that when I do present it and ask the participant to sign it, he or she will not be surprised by anything included on the form.

BUILDING THE PARTICIPANT POOL

Another primary purpose of the contact visit is to assess the appropriateness of a participant for the study. The major criterion for appropriateness is whether the subject of the researcher's study is central to the participant's experience. For example, a doctoral candidate wanting to study the way process writing affects an English teacher's experience in teaching writing must select English teachers for whom process writing plays a central role in their teaching.

As the interviewer speaks with potential participants, he or she can keep a record of those who seem most suitable, noting their key characteristics that are related to the subject of the study. Whether the interviewer asks participants to join the study at some point in the contact visit or gets back to them at a later date, he or she must remain aware of the character of the growing participant pool in order to be purposeful in the sampling. (See section on selecting participants later in this chapter.)

SOME LOGISTICAL CONSIDERATIONS

The experience of scheduling a contact visit often reflects what trying to schedule the actual interview with the participant will be like. If one is a reasonable process, the other is likely to be so too. If scheduling one contact visit is unduly frustrating, the interviewer may do well to take that into account in proceeding to build the participant pool.

Because of the time and energy required of both participants and interviewers, every step the interviewer takes to ease the logistics of the process is a step toward allowing the available energy to be focused on the interview itself. To facilitate communication, confirmation of appointments, and follow-up after the interviews, it is important for interviewers to develop a data base of their participants. They can use the contact visit to begin to collect data.

A simple participant information form can be of considerable use throughout the study. The form usually has two purposes: to facilitate communication between the interviewer and the participants; and to record basic data about the participant that will inform the final choice of participants and the reporting on the data later in the study. At minimum, the form should include the participants' home and work addresses and telephone numbers, the best time to be in touch with them, and the time to avoid calling them. Paying attention to the details of communications with participants from the beginning of the interview relationship can help in avoiding the mishaps of missed or confused appointments that can later plague an interview study.

The contact visit can also be used to determine the best times, places, and dates to interview potential participants. These are crucial. The place of the interview should be convenient to the participant, private, yet if at all possible familiar to him or her. It should be one in which the participant feels comfortable and secure. A public place such as a cafeteria or a coffee shop may seem convenient, but the noise, the lack of privacy, and the likelihood of the interview's becoming an event for others to comment upon undermine the effectiveness of such places for interviews.

If it can be determined at the time of the contact visit that a person would be an appropriate participant in the study, the interviewer can schedule time and dates right then. The interviewer should try to let the participant choose the hour, scheduling interviews within a time period consistent with the purpose of the three-interview structure as described in Chapter 2. Because each interview is meant to build on the preceding one, they are optimally spaced no more than a week and no less than a day apart.

In considering the time, dates, and place of interviews the prevailing principle must be equity. The participants are giving the interviewers something they want. The interviewers must be flexible enough to accommodate the participants' choice of location, time, and date. On the other hand, the interviewer also has constraints. Although equity necessitates flexibility, interviewers must also learn to set up interviews in such a way that they themselves are comfortable with the resulting schedule. Resentment on the part of either participant or interviewer will not bode well ultimately for the interviews.

After the contact visit, interviewers should write follow-up letters to the participants they select and to those they do not. The letters are used to thank the potential participants for meeting with the interviewers and, in the case of those who are selected for the study and who agree to participate, to confirm in writing the schedule of interview appointments.

Such detailed follow-up work in writing may seem onerous to the prospective interviewer; however, equity requires such consideration. In addition, this kind of step-by-step attention can have enormous practical benefits to the interviewer. Few things are more frustrating in an interview study than to drive a few hours to an appointment only to have the participant not show up. Sometimes the no-show is the result of poor communication. Sometimes it reflects a participant's lack of enthusiasm for the process because he or she feels asked to give a great deal while being offered very little consideration in return. In interviewing research, paying attention to the details of access and contact before the interviewing begins is the best investment interviewers can make as they select their participants and prepare to begin the interviews.

SELECTING PARTICIPANTS

Either during the contact process or shortly thereafter the researcher takes the crucial step of selecting the people he or she will interview. The purpose of an in-depth interview study is to understand the experience of those who are interviewed, not to predict or to control that experience. Because hypotheses are not being tested, the issue is not whether the researcher can generalize the finding of an interview study to a broader population. Instead the researcher's task is to present the experience of the people he or she interviews in compelling enough detail and in sufficient depth that those who read the study can connect to that experience, learn how it is constituted, and deepen their understanding of the issues it reflects. Because the basic assumptions underlying an interview study are different from those of an experimental study, selecting participants is approached differently.

"Only Connect"

The United States has more than 200,000 community college faculty. In our study of the work of community college faculty (Seidman, 1985) we could interview only 76 of them. The problem we faced was how to select those 76 participants so that what we learned about their experience would not be easily dismissed as idiosyncratic to them and irrelevant to a larger population. In their influential essay on experimental and quasi-experimental design, Campbell and Stanley (1963) call this the problem of external validity.

A conventional way of defining the issue is to ask whether what is learned from the interview sample can be generalized to the larger population. One step toward assuring generalizability is to select a sample that is representative of the larger population. The dominant approach to representativeness in experimental and quasi-experimental studies has been the random selection of participants. Theoretically, if a large enough sample is selected randomly or through a stratified, randomized approach, the resulting participant pool is not likely to be idiosyncratic.

In interview studies, however, it is not possible to employ random sampling or even a stratified random-sampling approach. Randomness is a statistical concept that depends on a very large number of participants. True randomness would be prohibitive in an in-depth interview study. Furthermore, interview participants must consent to be interviewed, so there is always an element of self-selection in an interview study. Self-selection and randomness are not compatible.

The job of an in-depth interviewer is to go to such depth in the interviews that surface considerations of representativeness and generalizability are replaced by a compelling evocation of an individual's experience. When this experience can be captured in depth, then two possibilities for making connections develop. They are the interview researcher's alternative to generalizability. (See Lincoln & Guba, 1985, for an extensive discussion of the concept of generalization.) First, the researcher may find connections among the experiences of the individuals he or she interviews. Such links among people whose individual lives are quite different but who are affected by common structural and social forces can help the reader see patterns in that experience. Those connections the researcher calls to the readers' attention for inspection and exploration.

Second, by presenting the stories of participants' experience, interviewers open up for readers the possibility of connecting their own stories to those presented in the study. In connecting, readers may not learn how to control or predict the experience being studied or their own, but they will understand better their complexities. They will appreciate more the intricate ways in which individual lives interact with social and structural forces and, perhaps, be more understanding and even humble in the face of those intricacies. Understanding and humility are not bad stances from which to try to effect improvement in education.

Purposeful Sampling

How best to select participants who will facilitate the ability of others to connect if random selection is not an option? The most commonly agreed upon answer is purposeful sampling. (See Patton, 1989.) Patton's discussion of purposeful-sampling techniques is very thoughtful. He suggests several approaches, including "typical case," "extreme or deviant case," "critical case," "sensitive case," "convenience" sampling, and "maximum variation" sampling (pp. 100–107).

Maximum variation sampling can refer to both sites and people (Tagg, 1985). The range of people and sites from which the people are selected should be fair to the larger population. This sampling technique should allow the widest possibility for readers of the study to connect to what they are reading. In my experience maximum variation sampling provides the most effective basic strategy for selecting participants for interview studies.

Consider, for example, a study in which the interviewer wants to explore the experience of minority teachers in local teachers' unions in urban school districts in Massachusetts (Galvan, 1990). Using the maximum variation approach, the researcher would analyze the potential population to assess the maximum range of sites and people that constitute the population.

First she would have to define what she meant by the term *urban*. Then she would have to determine the range of school systems in Massachusetts that fall within her definition. Within the systems she would have to decide whether she were interested in the experience of all minority teachers, those in grades K–12, or just those in some particular grade level.

In Massachusetts, local teachers' unions are usually affiliated with either the National Education Association or the American Federation of Teachers. She would have to decide whether she were interested in studying the experience of minority teachers affiliated with both unions or with just one.

After considering the range of sites, she would then have to consider the range of people who are minority teachers and belong to local teachers' unions. She would have to determine the relative number of male and female minority teachers, the range of ethnic groups represented, the range of subject matter they teach, their levels of teaching, and the age and experience of teachers represented in the larger population.

The above characteristics are illustrative but not exhaustive of the range of variations present in the population whose experience this researcher might want to try to understand. If the range became unmanageable, the researcher would want to limit the study, looking at, for example, the experience of one minority group in a number of locals or the experience of the full range of minority members in one or two locals. The goal would remain to sample purposely the widest variation of sites and people within the limits of the study.

In addition to selecting participants who reflect the wide range in the larger population under study, another useful approach is to select some participants who are outside that range and may in some sense be considered negative cases (Lincoln & Guba, 1985). In the study discussed above about what it is like for a minority teacher to be a member of a teachers' union, it would also be useful to include some nonminority teachers who are also members of the local. If the researcher discovers through interviews that nonminority and minority teachers are having similar experiences, then the researcher will know that some issues may not be a matter of ethnicity or race.

As another example, Schatzkamer (1986) was interested in studying the experience of older women returning to community colleges. She also decided to interview some older men who were returning to college to see in what ways their experience connected to that of the women in her sample. Selecting participants to interview who are outside the range of those at the center of the study is an effective way for interviewers to check themselves against drawing easy conclusions from their research.

SNARES TO AVOID IN THE SELECTION PROCESS

New interviewers may take too personally a potential participant's reluctance to get involved. It does little good to try to persuade such a person to participate in an interview she or he would rather not do. In the face of initial reluctance, interviewers may go to great lengths to exercise persuasion only to find later the interview itself to be an ongoing struggle (Richardson et al., 1965). The interviewer must strike a balance between too easily accepting a quick expression of disinterest from a potential participant and too ardently trying to persuade a reluctant one that she or he really is not disinclined to participate.

Another snare is the potential participant who is too eager to be interviewed. During the contact visit an interviewer can ascertain whether the person has some ax to grind. In a contact visit Sullivan and I made to one community college, we learned that the college had just dismissed its president. The school was divided into factions: those who had worked for the president's dismissal and those who had not. Some of the faculty we contacted were very reluctant to get involved in an interview. Others were too eager. The purpose of our study was understanding the work of community college faculty. Although it is true that academic politics are a part of that work, in this particular case the partisan politics of the campus threatened to load our study with interview participants inclined to be more like informers (Dean & Whyte, 1958; Lincoln & Guba, 1985; Richardson et al., 1965).

On occasion during a contact visit, someone would tell us we must interview a colleague who won an award and would be wonderful to talk to. Our instinct was always to avoid such "stars." The method of in-depth interviewing elicits people's stories in a way that shows each person to be interesting no matter how anonymous.

HOW MANY PARTICIPANTS ARE ENOUGH?

New interviewers frequently ask how many participants they must have in their study. Some researchers argue for an emerging research design in which the number of participants in a study is not established ahead of time. New participants are added as new dimensions of the issues become apparent through earlier interviews (Lincoln & Guba, 1985). Other researchers discuss a "snowballing" approach to selecting participants, in which one participant leads to another (Bertaux, 1981). But even if researchers use a purposeful sampling technique designed to gain maximum variation and then add to their sample through a snowballing process, they must know when they have interviewed enough participants.

There are two criteria for enough. The first is sufficiency. Are there sufficient numbers to reflect the range of participants and sites that make up the population so that others outside the sample might have a chance to connect to the experiences of those in it? In our community college study, we had to have enough participants to reflect vocational and liberal arts faculty, men, women, and minorities, and age and experience ranges. We also considered faculty with advanced degrees and without degrees. In addition, we were reluctant to interview only one person in any particular category.

The other criterion is saturation of information. A number of writers (Douglas, 1976; Glaser & Strauss, 1967; Lincoln & Guba, 1985) discuss a point in a study at which the interviewer begins to hear the same information reported. He or she is no longer learning anything new. Douglas (1985) is even bold enough to attempt to assess when that began to happen in his studies. If he had to pick a number, he said, it would be 25 participants.

I would be reluctant to establish such a number. "Enough" is an interactive reflection of every step of the interview process and different for each study and each researcher. The criteria of sufficiency and saturation are useful, but practical exigencies of time, money, and other resources also play a role, especially in doctoral research.

The method of in-depth, phenomenological interviewing applied to a sample of participants who all experience similar structural and social conditions gives enormous power to the stories of a relatively few participants. Researchers can figure out ahead of time the range of sites and people that they would like to sample and set a goal for a certain number of participants in the study. At some point, however, the interviewer may recognize that he or she is not learning anything decidedly new and that the process of interviewing itself is becoming laborious rather than pleasurable (Bertaux, 1981). That is a time to say "enough."

5

Affirming
Informed Consent

First-time interviewers tend to be hesitant about securing their participants' informed, written consent to be interviewed. Some interviewers
worry that telling people what they are studying will skew the results of
their study. They also tend to minimize participants' sense of risk at being
involved in an interview. The interviewers have no doubt about their
own good intentions, but they do not anticipate the type of material that
can be generated in an in-depth interview.

In-depth interviews ask participants to reconstruct their life history
as it relates to the subject of inquiry. In the process, a measure of intimacy
can develop between interviewers and participants that leads the participants to share aspects of their lives that, if misused, could leave them
extremely vulnerable. Participants have the right to be protected against
such vulnerability. Furthermore, interviewers can protect themselves
against misunderstanding through the process of seeking informed consent, which requires them to be explicit about the range and purpose of
their study in a way that makes them be clear about what they are doing.
Finally, given the extensiveness of the interview process and the method
of following up on what the participants have to say (see Chapter 6),
providing people ahead of time with as much information as possible
about each aspect of the study is not likely to skew the results of 4½ hours
of interviewing.

The relatively recent impetus toward protecting rights of research
participants stems from the reaction to the disregard for human dignity
perpetrated during World War II by researchers in concentration camps
controlled by Nazi Germany. The Nuremburg trials resulted in the Nuremburg Code adopted by the United Nations General Assembly in 1946,

which stated that "the voluntary consent of the human subject is absolutely essential" (Reynolds, 1979, p. 436).

After World War II, federal guidelines concerning the protection of the rights of human subjects were issued in the 1950s, 1960s, 1970s, and 1980s. (See Applebaum, Lidz, & Meisel, 1987; Faden & Beauchamp, 1986.) The guidelines were originally applied broadly to all research supported directly by federal funds and to all that conducted in institutions receiving federal funds.

That broad interpretation was narrowed significantly in 1981 (Reynolds, 1982) to cover only the former. However, most institutions of higher education, in order to demonstrate to the federal government their adherence to the spirit and intent of federal guidelines, continue to require informed consent in all research involving human subjects unless no risk is involved.

Interviewing research is legally exempted from the requirement of informed consent unless all the following conditions exist:

(i) Responses are recorded in such a manner that the human subjects can be identified, directly or through identifiers linked to the subject; (ii) the subject's responses, if they became known outside the research, could reasonably place the subject at risk of criminal or civil liability or be damaging to the subject's financial standing or employability; and (iii) the research deals with sensitive aspects of the subject's own behavior such as illegal conduct, drug use, sexual behavior, or use of alcohol. (Department of Health and Human Services, 1981)

The basic federal policy presupposed a survey type of interviewing in which the identity of the participant is not known, the data collected are not sensitive, and no harm can be envisioned for the participants (Reynolds, 1982). In-depth interviewing, however, cannot be likened to routine survey interviewing. First, the topic of inquiry, no matter how apparently innocent, is placed within the total life context of the participant. That contextual exploration is likely to raise sensitive issues. Second, the interviews are recorded and the identity of the participant, even disguised, is potentially discernible by someone who knows him or her. Third, the potential vulnerability of the participant cannot be calculated ahead of time.

For these reasons, even though an interviewer's research may not be funded by federal sources and informed consent of participants is therefore not legally necessary, it is both ethically and methodologically desirable to seek it. The consent of the participant is most effectively indicated by his or her signature on an informed consent form.

The consent form should cover the following main points:

1. It should tell the participants what they are being asked to do, by whom, and for what purpose. Participants must know the identity of the researcher, his or her affiliations if any, and whom to contact for information if they have problems with the research process.
2. It should inform the participants of any risks they might be taking by participating in the research.
3. It should inform the participants what rights they have in the process, particularly the right of review of material and the right to withdraw from the process.
4. It should indicate whether or not participants' names will be used in the study, whether any other names will be used, or whether pseudonyms will be substituted.
5. It should indicate how the results of the study will be disseminated and whether participants can expect to benefit in any way, monetarily or otherwise, from participating in the study.
6. It should indicate that participants are free to participate or not participate in the research without prejudice to them.
7. In the case of children, it must be signed by the child's legal guardian. Children cannot be expected to give totally informed consent. (Department of Health and Human Services, 1981)

ISSUES IN INFORMED CONSENT

The Right to Know

In the second of the three interviews, interviewers ask participants to reconstruct the details of their experience within the subject area being studied. Students talking about their experiences in classes, and teachers, counselors, and administrators talking about their experiences at work have the right to be told explicitly with whom the interview material will be shared and in what forum it will be disseminated. Moreover, researchers have an obligation to structure their research process so that they will not be likely to share raw interview data with anyone who would be in a position to capitalize on the information or to make participants vulnerable as a result.

I always suggest to doctoral candidates that they cast the widest net they think possible in outlining the various uses they will make of information collected. On first instinct, many students limit the intended use to their dissertation. This means that if they later decide to publish something from their dissertation, or to base a presentation for a conference on their research, they will then be obligated to go back to their participants to seek additional permission to use the material in ways not originally listed in the consent form.

Confidentiality and Legal Status of Data

Participants also have a right to know in what form material from their interviews will be shared with the public. I have often seen drafts of written consent forms in which interviewers promise that the material they gather will be kept confidential. Although it may be possible in medical or survey research to keep individual responses confidential and to report only in aggregate terms, such a promise is inconsistent with the purpose and method of in-depth interviewing research. Most people who interview do so because they want to make the experience of individuals accessible to others. In addition, research information is not privileged and is thereby subject to subpoena by the courts (Reynolds, 1979).

The first of the Principles of Professional Responsibility of the American Anthropological Association states that in research,

> In research, anthropologists' paramount responsibility is to those they study. When there is a conflict of interest, these individuals must come first. Anthropologists must do everything in their power to protect the physical, social, and psychological welfare and to honor the dignity and privacy of those studied. (American Anthropological Association, 1983, p. 1)

When we were doing our study of community college faculty, we interviewed a small number of students to understand how their experience related to what the faculty were telling us. In one of the interviews, a student participant revealed that he occasionally sold drugs on the campus. Our research team discussed the situation. We knew that legally we could not keep the information confidential; nor ethically could we make the participant vulnerable through his participation in our research.

We were in a very uncomfortable position. Although it was not likely to happen, this particular person might be arrested and our interview data somehow subpoenaed and used against him. Though we did not condone his pushing marijuana on the campus, we would not have known of it through any way other than our interviews. We did not feel that we could make him more vulnerable than he already was as a result of participating in our study. As interesting as the story he was telling us was, we decided that the best course of action was to terminate the interviews and destroy the tapes. It was not an altogether comfortable resolution.

The Extensive Use of Interview Data

In Chapter 8, I discuss ways of working with the material and disseminating it. Suffice it to say here that the intent of this type of interviewing is to use as much as possible the words of the participants to illuminate the experience they are reconstructing in their interviews.

A conventional expectation participants have is that researchers use quotations from interviews. But in reporting on in-depth interviewing, researchers include lengthy excerpts from interview transcripts rather than short quotations. As an element of informed consent, participants have the right to know how extensively the interviewer might use the data from his or her interview.

Anonymity

Such extensive use of participants' words leads to one of the central issues in informed consent, that of anonymity. The standard assumption is that participants in in-depth interview studies will remain anonymous. That assumption has implications for interviewers from the moment they start their research. In their proposals, for instance, which are usually public and accessible documents, they should avoid listing names of sites or of people that could be traced later when the research is completed.

Interviewers working with in-depth interview material, however, cannot guarantee anonymity. The center of the research is the experience of the participants, gathered within the context of their lives. Because a considerable part of that experience may be shared in the research report, a reader who knows the participant may recognize him or her.

Nonetheless, the interviewer can work to protect the anonymity of the participant and can say how that will be done in the written consent form. For example, the participant has the right to know who will transcribe the interview audiotapes. If it is not to be the interviewer, the interviewer can tell what steps will be taken to assure that the transcriber does not misuse information about the identity of the participant. Second, the participant can be assured that transcriptions will contain only initials for all proper names, so that even if a casual reader were somehow to see the transcripts, no proper names would be present. Third, the interviewer can promise to use pseudonyms in the final report. Fourth, in some cases the interviewer can choose to actively disguise the participant's identity.

In her study *The Contextual Realities of Being a Lesbian Physical Educator: Living in Two Worlds*, Woods (1990) was concerned that her participants would be vulnerable if they could be identified. As part of her written consent form, she made the following statement and outlined the steps that she would take to protect — but not guarantee — her participants' anonymity:

> In a study of this nature, the anonymity of participants is a priority. Although anonymity can not be fully guaranteed, the following are steps taken at each stage of the research process to protect your anonymity.
> A. Access to participants has been gained in two ways: (a) my personal contacts; and (b) contacts given by those being interviewed. All initial contacts with a potential participant will be made by the person or participant suggesting the teacher to be interviewed. I will contact the potential participant directly only if she has agreed to discuss the possibility of being interviewed.
> B. All interviews will take place in a safe space to be designated by the participant.
> C. The researcher will not interview more than one teacher employed in a single district.
> D. With the exception of the dissertation committee chairperson, I will not discuss with the dissertation committee or anyone else any names, teaching locations or identifying particulars of the participants.
> E. Interview transcripts may be completed by two persons: (a) myself; and/or (b) a reputable and discrete transcriber. If someone other than myself transcribes the audio tapes, I will erase from the audio-tapes all names and identifying particulars before submitting them for transcription.
> F. As stated, pseudonyms will be substituted in the transcripts for all names of persons, schools, school districts, cities, towns, and counties. Every step will be taken to adequately disguise the participant's identity and teaching location in any published materials or presentations.
> G. The transcripts will remain in the direct physical possession of the researcher. All audio-tapes and consent forms are kept in a safety deposit box. Tapes will be destroyed upon acceptance of the dissertation or, at your request, will be returned to you. (p. 224)

Woods felt that her participants might be taking risks by participating in her study. To protect them and to establish conditions in which they would feel safe to talk, she devised the most effective and practical means she could to minimize those risks. Although I was concerned about her promise to destroy the audiotapes of the interviews, the care she took to protect her participants' identity without guaranteeing them anonymity, and her explicitness with potential participants, seemed to me a model of forthrightness.

As Woods indicates, if the likelihood of a participant's being identi-fied is high, and if being so identified would make him or her vulnerable, it may be best to disguise the person's identity. This measure, which is more active than giving the participant a pseudonym, might involve changing the location in which the person resides or the specific nature of the activity being reconstructed. For example, in *In the Words of the Faculty* (Seidman, 1985), I changed the state in which one participant taught as well as the subject she taught. The guidelines the researcher must use in judging the appropriateness of such changes are whether the likelihood of a participant's being identified is high, whether he or she would be made vulnerable if identified, and whether the disguise can be effected in a way that does not distort the data.

Informed consent assumes but does not require anonymity (Reyn-olds, 1979). What it does require is that the participants be informed, before the interviews begin, as to whether steps will be taken to protect their identity. At least one writer (Mishler, 1986), however, argues that anonymity is not automatically a good thing and that participants should be given the choice as to whether they wish their names to be used. My experience leads me to suggest that interviews be conducted under the assumption that the interviewer will take steps to protect the anonymity of the participants. After the interview is completed, the participants will be in a better position to judge whether they wish to conceal their identities.

Sponsorship

If the study is sponsored in any way, that sponsorship should be made clear to participants. Sponsorship may range from a school system's endorsement of and interest in the results to active financial support of the research. No matter where on the continuum the support falls, the interviewer has an obligation to inform the participant of the nature of the sponsorship. The participant must be free to engage or not to engage in the research knowing who else is interested in it and to what possible uses it might be put.

Remuneration

A major issue is whether the participant can expect any remunera-tion for the interviews. Such remuneration could range from pay on a per-interview basis to the promise that if the interviews lead to commer-cial publication, the participant would have the right to some proportion of the royalties. The issue is a complicated one. Anything more than a

token payment would seriously threaten to bias the potential participants' motivation for taking part in the study. On the other hand, some
researchers see interviewers as potentially expropriating the words of the
participants for their own uses in an exploitative manner (Patai, 1987).
Establishing an equitable percentage of royalties to allocate to a participant, given all the hours of work that go into an interview study before
and after the actual interview, is complicated. Except in the case of a
best seller, a percentage of royalties may not make much financial sense.

In the studies I have conducted, I have not offered remuneration to
the participants. At the conclusion of an interview, I normally present
a token of my appreciation. I think there are other levels of reciprocity
that occur in the interview process that can substitute for financial remu
neration. Participants have told me and my research associates that the
occasion of their interview was the first time anybody had ever sat down
to talk about their work with them. Participants have said that they
appreciated being listened to and that participating in the interviews was
an important experience for them.

Each interviewer has to figure out for him or herself the issue of
remuneration. Whatever he or she decides should be explicit in the written consent form. It should state clearly either that the participant is
agreeing not to make any financial claim upon the interviewer or what
the basis of the remuneration will be. Inequity and certainly discomfort
are more likely to arise from an unclear position about the issue of money
than from a clear decision either to remunerate or not. The principle
should be to give the participant the opportunity to join or not to join
the study on the basis of explicit information.

Right of Withdrawal and Review

The three 90-minute interviews are designed to build a framework
for a relationship between the interviewer and the participant that is
equitable and leads to a reasonable level of trust between the two. The
intimate process of a participant's placing experience in the context of his
or her life and meeting repeatedly over a period of a few weeks for
discussion may lead a participant to divulge information that he or she
later regrets sharing. The researcher must make clear that the participant
has the right to withdraw from the study at any time during the interviews or within a specified time after they are completed. In addition,
the participant must have the right to withhold any part of the interview
data he or she chooses.

What is less clear is what right the participant has to review and
approve the way the interviewer has worked with the material gathered

in the study. The interviewer may well choose to work out a way for the participant to have access to both the raw data and the way he or she has worked with that information in writing up the study. Interviewers may offer to share copies of the audiotapes or transcriptions of those tapes. Such sharing would facilitate the participant's ability to review the interview experience and to decide whether to ask the interviewer not to use certain parts of the material.

Finally, interviewers may offer to share the entire report before publication or the parts of the final report that most concern a participant. Some scholars of qualitative research consider this step to be crucial for the credibility of the study (Lincoln & Guba, 1985). In the interview work I have done, I have often used extensive profiles of the participants crafted in their own words from the interview transcripts. When I have made a profile from a participant's experience, I contact the person and offer to share the profile with her or him before I disseminate it. If the participant asks to review the profile, I send it. I do so with the stipulation that I want to know if it contains anything inaccurate or unfair to the larger interview. I also want to know if there is anything in the profile with which the participant is uncomfortable.

Although I would not disseminate anything that a participant told me at this stage would make him or her vulnerable, neither would I give the person automatic censure on matters of interpretation. One participant in our community college study asked me to delete a portion of the profile I had developed of him, in his own words, in which he said that he was not proud of working at his community college. I agreed to delete the passage to which he was referring because he felt that it could make him vulnerable if he were identified. But later in an interpretive section of the study, not tied to any single participant, I discussed the issue of community college faculty's sense of status in their jobs, keeping what that participant had told me in mind.

At some point the interviewer-researcher has to become responsible for what he or she writes. In this instance, I felt somewhat compromised in taking that responsibility because the participant had asked me to delete important information that had informed part of my analysis. On the other hand, I was committed to preserving the dignity of participants and not making them vulnerable as a result of their participation in the study. As in many other aspects of interviewing research, the researcher has to balance conflicting claims. Although the American Anthropological Association's first principle gives guidance on how to execute that balancing act, it does not make keeping one's balance any easier. The interviewer must be willing to take ownership of the material and be responsible for the consequences. I do not think the researcher can shift the burden of that responsibility to the participant, and yet the participant has an interest in how the researcher carries it out.

Whatever the interviewer decides to do about the participant's rights of review, as in the case of remuneration, the most important point is to be explicit. Inequity in interviewing results more often from a researcher's being unclear about the framework within which interviewer and participant are working than from any decision on a specific issue. (For an interesting discussion of what can happen when an interviewer does clarify the responsibility she intended to take for the interviewing material, see Lightfoot, 1983.)

AFFIRMING WRITTEN CONSENT

When guidelines for seeking informed consent were first issued in the 1960s and 1970s by federal agencies, many researchers saw the benefits, but some felt that the costs outweighed them. My own sense is that in interviewing studies, there is everything to be gained by seeking informed consent and nothing to lose. In addition to the ethical considerations, the most distinct advantage is that developing the written consent form requires that interviewers think through the structure and processes of their study, making them explicit not only to their participants but to themselves. Developing a satisfactory written consent form requires that interviewers be clear about their purposes, methods, and relationship with their participants. In addition to allowing the potential participant to decide whether to participate in the study on the basis of sufficient information, the informed consent form serves as a contract of sorts, which can also protect interviewers in cases of misunderstanding. Its clarity can lead a researcher to a more equitable relationship with participants and to the increased effectiveness that almost always flows from equity.

6

Technique Isn't Everything, But It Is a Lot

It is tempting to say that interviewing is an art, a reflection of the personality of the interviewer, and cannot be taught. This line of thinking implies that either you are good at it or you are not. But that is only half true. Researchers can learn techniques and skills of interviewing. What follows is a discussion of those skills as I have come to understand them from my own experience of interviewing and that of others.

LISTEN MORE, TALK LESS

Listening is the most important skill in interviewing. The hardest work for most interviewers is to keep quiet and to listen actively. In contrast to many books about interviewing that concentrate on the types of questions that interviewers ask, I want to start this chapter by talking about the type of listening the interviewer must do.

Interviewers must listen on at least three levels. First, they must listen to what the participant is saying. They must concentrate on the substance to make sure that they understand it and to assess whether what they are hearing is as detailed and complete as they would like it to be. They must concentrate so that they internalize what participants say. Later, interviewers' questions will often flow from this earlier listening.

On a second level, interviewers must listen for what George Steiner (1978) calls "inner voice," as opposed to an outer, more public voice. An outer, or public, voice always reflects an awareness of the audience. It is not untrue; it is guarded. It is a voice that participants would use if they were talking to an audience of 300 in an auditorium.

There is a language of the outer voice to which interviewers can become sensitive. For example, whenever I hear participants talk about the problems they are facing as a "challenge" or their work as an "adventure," I sense that I am hearing a public voice, and I search for ways to get to the inner voice. "Challenge" and "adventure" convey the positive aspects of a participant's grappling with a difficult experience but not the struggle. Another word that attracts my attention is "fascinate." I often hear that word on talk-show interviews; it usually works to communicate some sort of interest while covering up its exact nature. Whenever I hear a participant use "fascinate," I ask for elucidation. By taking participants' language seriously without making them feel defensive about it, interviewers can encourage a level of thoughtfulness more characteristic of inner voice.

On a third level, interviewers — like good teachers in a classroom — must listen while remaining aware of the process as well as the substance. They must be conscious of time during the interview; they must be aware of how much has been covered and how much there is yet to go. They must be sensitive to the participant's energy level and any nonverbal cues he or she may be offering. Interviewers must listen hard to assess the progress of the interview and to stay alert for cues about how to move the interview forward as necessary.

This type of active listening requires concentration and focus beyond that we usually do in everyday life. It requires that, for a good part of the time, we quash our normal instinct to talk. At the same time, interviewers must be ready to say something when a navigational nudge is needed.

In order to facilitate active listening, in addition to tape recording the interview, interviewers can take notes. These working notes help interviewers concentrate on what the participant is saying. They also help to keep interviewers from interrupting the participant by allowing them to keep track of things that the participant has mentioned and come back to them when the timing is right.

A good way to gauge listening skills is to transcribe an interview tape. Separate the interviewer's questions from the participant's responses by new paragraphs. Compare the relative length of the participant's paragraphs with the interviewer's. If the interviewer is listening well, his or her paragraphs will be short, relatively infrequently interspersed among longer paragraphs of the participant's responses.

Note the following one-page transcript, for example. It is taken from the beginning of interview number two on the experience of being an instructional designer.

INTERVIEWER: Could you tell me as much as possible about the details of your experience at work as an instructional designer presently or as a grad student working in the area of instructional design?

PARTICIPANT: The details of instructional design . . . O.K.

INTERVIEWER: Your present experience . . .

PARTICIPANT: Yeah.

INTERVIEWER: As an instructional designer.

PARTICIPANT: Umh . . . So something like . . . you mean something like perhaps the last several jobs I've done?

INTERVIEWER: No, what you're presently doing, like as a student maybe right now or you said you did have a job that you're working on.

PARTICIPANT: Yeah, well, I have one current, current job umh, the thing is that when you said current I may or may in any given day, I may or may not happen to have a job; you know they just, they just fall out of the sky. You don't really — My experience in getting work has been that — no matter what I do to try to get work I don't see any direct results between those efforts and getting the jobs, right. On the other hand, I do get jobs. They just fall out of the sky [laugh]. All I can say about you know like meteorites. Unh, and they range over a wide, wide variety of — of contact. Umh, [sniffle] it could be teaching office workers how to use software. I've done all of those, all of those kinds of things. Umh, and typically the things start through the proposal, umh less and less I've been doing the actual proposals, but usually I'm not ah — the actual getting the business is not my job and somewhere there is a line between; writing the proposal is part of getting the business and um so I usually have something to do with writing the proposal but I don't do a lot of getting the business. Umh [sniffle] somewhere after the proposal is written or during the proposal stage I'm brought in [sniffle] — and I get to do the work. (Tremblay, 1990)

This text is a good example of an interviewer's listening hard to a participant. At the beginning of the interview, the participant is not quite focused. The interviewer, concentrating on what he is saying, nudges him into the frame of reference of the second interview. Once she has the participant in the right channel, she listens and lets him talk. Even when the participant pauses for a few seconds, she does not interrupt.

Patai (1987) describes the process of listening to her Brazilian women participants as an intense form of concentration and openness to them that led her to become absorbed in them (p. 12). Although not every interview takes on the almost magical quality that Patai describes, interest in the participant's experience and a willingness to hold one's own ego in check are keys to the hard work of listening in an interview that leads to the type of absorption Patai describes.

FOLLOW UP ON WHAT THE PARTICIPANT SAYS

When interviewers do talk in an interview, they usually ask questions. The key to asking questions during in-depth interviewing is to let them follow, as much as possible, from what the participant is saying. Although the interviewer comes to each interview with a basic question that establishes the purpose and focus of the interview, it is in response to what the participant says that the interviewer follows up, asks for clarification, seeks concrete details, and requests stories. Rather than preparing a preset interview guide, the interviewer's basic work in this approach to interviewing is to listen actively and to move the interview forward as much as possible by building on what the participant has begun to share.

ASK QUESTIONS WHEN YOU DO NOT UNDERSTAND

It is hard work to understand everything people say. Sometimes the context is not clear. At other times we do not understand the specific referent of what someone is saying. In everyday conversation we often let such things slide by without understanding them. In interviewing such sliding undermines the process.

The interview structure is cumulative. One interview establishes the context for the next. Not having understood something in an early interview, an interviewer might miss the significance of something a participant says later. Passages in interviews become links to each other in ways that cannot be foretold. Also, the interviewer who lets a participant know when he or she does not understand something shows the person that the interviewer is listening.

Sometimes it is difficult to get the chronology of an experience straight. It is important for interviewers to understand experiences in the context of time. A question like, "Can you tell me again when that happened?" is a reasonable one. I use the word *again* so as not to imply to participants that they are not being clear, thereby making them defensive, but rather, as is often the case, to suggest that I was just not attentive enough the first time around.

Sometimes participants use vague words that seem to be communicating but are not explicit. For example, one community college faculty member whom I interviewed consistently described his students by saying, "They are very nice." I did not know what he meant by the term *nice*. In a way it seemed to trivialize the respect for his students that he had communicated throughout the interview. I asked him, "What is *nice*?" He said,

> The students at the private university [where he had previously taught] were rude, and they were frequently demanding. I don't mean intellectually demanding. They would say, "You didn't say that. You didn't say you were going to test us on that sort of thing." Our students at the community college are really nice. I realize this sounds silly; I apologize for it. It really sounds crazy to say for some reason we happen to have the nicest people around that happen to live in this neighborhood. Now that's not likely. But we have an attitude on this campus. There is a kind of mutual respect and I get a lot of this when our students come back after they have gone somewhere else. . . . There is a different feeling, even though it is a bigger school, and you really don't know everybody. Uh, nonetheless there is a kind of community feeling here and there is a lack of what I call a mean spirit where you are just touchy and aggressive and, uh, inquisitive. Maybe our students are not that motivated; maybe that's why they are not; but they are really nice to teach. You almost never have anything you could call a discipline problem. It just doesn't happen. . . . I don't know; I do like our students. I think it would be absolutely perfect if they were a little better prepared, but that's not as important as being nice people. . . . They are the kind of people that are pleasant to work with. (Seidman et al., 1983)

In responding to my request for clarification about his use of the word *nice*, the participant went more deeply into the nature of his teaching experience. By my taking his language seriously, he explored what he meant when he used the word *nice*. As the interviewer, I then understood better what, for him, were the complexities implied in his use of the apparently simple word *nice*.

ASK TO HEAR MORE ABOUT A SUBJECT

When an interviewer wants to hear more about what a participant is saying, he or she should trust that instinct. Interviewers should ask questions when they feel unsatisfied with what they have heard. Sometimes they do not think that they have heard the entire story; other times they may think that they are getting generalities and they want to hear the details; or they may just be interested in what the participant is saying and want to hear more. Sometimes when listening, interviewers begin to feel a vague question welling up inside them because they sense there is more to the story. In those instances it is important for them to ask to hear more.

For example, in a study of older women returning to community colleges (Schatzkamer, 1986), one student spoke about her experience in a math course. The last two-thirds of the technical math course she was taking was devoted to calculus.

She said, "At that point, I capsized. That was beyond the capacities of my math . . . it was beyond me. So I was obedient. This is something I don't usually do in school, but I just memorized and did what I was told and followed out the formulas the way I was told I should and which I regret. I got an A, but I regret it."

The interviewer, hearing the phrase "I regret it," wanted to hear more. She asked, based on what the participant had said, "What do you regret?"

The participant responded, "I never really understood it, you know. I didn't really learn. I'm sure there is something lovely there under all that calculus to be learned and I didn't learn that. I theoretically learned how to use it as a tool. By being slavish you know: plugging numbers into formulas and finding the right formula and stuff; that's not the way math should be learned and it's not really understanding."

By following up on the participant's phrase of regret, the interviewer gave the participant a chance to go a step further in her story. In so doing she revealed a desire to learn and a potential appreciation for the beauty of math that increases the reader's understanding of her community college experience and our respect for her as an individual.

EXPLORE, DON'T PROBE

In referring to the skill of following up on what participants say, the literature on interviewing often uses the word *probe*. (See, e.g., Lincoln & Guba, 1985.) I have never been comfortable with that word. I always think of a sharp instrument pressing on soft flesh when I hear it. The word also conveys a sense of the powerful interviewer treating the participant as an object. I am more comfortable with the notion of exploring with the participant than with probing into what the participant says.

At the same time, too much and ill-timed exploration of the participant's words can make him or her defensive and shift the meaning-making from the participant to the interviewer. The interview can become too easily a vehicle for the interviewer's agenda rather than an exploration of the participant's experience. Too little exploration, however, can leave an interviewer unsure of the participant's meaning in the material he or she has gathered. It can also leave the participant using abstractions and generalities that are not useful (Hyman et al., 1954).

LISTEN MORE, TALK LESS, AND ASK REAL QUESTIONS

Listen more, talk less. I repeat the first law of interviewing here for emphasis and because it is so easy to forget. When you do ask questions, ask only real questions. By a real question I mean one to which the interviewer does not already know or anticipate the response. If interviewers want to ask a question to which they think they know the response, it would be better to say what they think, and then to ask the participant what he or she thinks of the assertion.

AVOID LEADING QUESTIONS

A leading question is one that influences the direction the response will take. Sometimes the lead is in the intonation of the question: The tone implies an expectation. Sometimes it is in the wording, syntax, and intonation of the question, as when an interviewer asks, "Did you *really* mean to do that?" Sometimes the lead is in the conclusion implied by the question. One interviewer, listening to a participant's story about her family and her early schooling, asked: "Your parents pushed you to study, didn't they?" Or in another place, the interviewer asked, "How satisfied were you with your student teaching placement?" instead of, for example, "What was your student teaching placement like for you?" (For a more extensive discussion of leading questions, see Patton, 1989; Richardson et al., 1965.)

ASK OPEN-ENDED QUESTIONS

An open-ended question, unlike a leading question, establishes the territory to be explored while allowing the participant to take any direction he or she wants. It does not presume an answer. There are at least two types of open-ended questions especially relevant to in-depth interviewing. One is what Spradley (1979) calls the "grand tour" question (pp. 86–87), in which the interviewer asks the participant to reconstruct a significant segment of an experience. For example, in interviewing a counselor, an interviewer might say, "Take me through a day in your work life." Or in working with a student teacher, an interviewer might ask, "Reconstruct your day for me from the time you wake up to the time you go to bed."

There is also the mini-tour, in which the interviewer asks the participant to reconstruct the details of a more limited time span or of a particular experience. For example, an interviewer might ask a vice principal to reconstruct the details of a particular disciplinary session with a student; or an interviewer might ask a teacher to talk about the experience of a particular conference with a parent.

A second type of open-ended question focuses more on the subjective experience of the participant than on the external structure. For example, a participant might begin to talk about her experience in a parent conference. After asking her what happened at the conference, the interviewer might ask her to talk about what that conference was like for her.

Although there are many approaches to open-ended questioning, when I am interested in understanding the participant's subjective experience, I often find myself asking the question, "What was that like for you?" As Schutz (1967) indicated, it is not possible to experience what the participant experienced. If we could, then we would be the participant. Perhaps the closest we can come is to ask the metaphorical question implied in the word *like*. When interviewers ask what something was like for participants, they are giving them the chance to reconstruct their experience according to their own sense of what was important, unguided by the interviewer.

FOLLOW UP, DON'T INTERRUPT

Avoid interrupting participants when they are talking. Often an interviewer is more interested in something a participant says than the speaker seems to be. While the participant continues talking, the interviewer feels strongly tempted to interrupt to pursue the interesting point. Rather than doing so, however, the interviewer can jot down the key word and follow up on it later, when doing so will not interrupt the participant's train of thought. The opportunity may come later in the same interview or even in a subsequent one (Richardson et al., 1965).

Once, for example, a teacher had been talking early in the second interview about the frenetic pace of her day and about having no place to hide. At the time, I was very interested in what she said, but she went right on to other aspects of her experience. Rather than interrupting her then, I wrote down in my working notes the phrases "frenetic pace" and "no place to hide."

Later, when there was a pause in her responses, I returned to those phrases by saying, "A while back you talked about a very frenetic pace. You talked about coming in the door, teaching your class, walking to your office, keeping extensive hours, having no place to hide. Would you talk more about that frenetic pace and having no place to hide?" [Richardson et al., 1965, term this approach "the echo" (pp. 157–163) and caution against its overuse.]

The participant responded by talking about the effect of her community college's architecture on her daily life. In order to make faculty as accessible as possible to students, the designers of her campus had made the wall of faculty offices that faced the hallway of glass. The participant spoke about her frustration with never having a place to go in her building where she could get some work done without being seen and, most likely, interrupted. Although she could close the door of her office, she could never close out those who sought her.

ASK PARTICIPANTS TO TALK TO YOU AS IF YOU WERE SOMEONE ELSE

Every interviewer probably develops favorite approaches to participants. I have two to which I return often. The first I use when I sense that I am hearing a public voice and I am searching for an inner one (see above). In those situations, I often use what Patton calls role-playing questions. (Patton, 1989; also see Spradley, 1979.) I try to figure out the person with whom the participant might be most comfortable talking personally. I then try asking the participant to imagine that I am that person.

I might say, "If I were your spouse (or your father, or your teacher, or your friend), what would you say to me?" Sometimes this question falls flat. I am unable to shift the participant's frame of reference enough so that he or she talks to me as though I were someone else. But often, if used sparingly, the role-playing approach works. The participant takes on a different voice, becomes animated in a way that he or she has not been until then, and both the participant and I enjoy for a few moments the new roles that we have assumed.

ASK PARTICIPANTS TO TELL A STORY

I also often ask participants to tell me a story about what they are discussing. In a sense, everything said in an interview is a story. But if a participant were talking about, for example, relationships with students, I might ask for a story about one particular student who stands out in his or her experience.

Not everybody is comfortable with being asked directly to tell a story. The request seems to block people who may think they do not tell good stories or that story telling is something only other people do. Others, however, suddenly remember a particular incident, become deeply engrossed in reconstructing it, and tell a wonderful story that conveys their experience as concretely as anything could.

I will always remember the story one student teacher told when she was describing the trouble she was having figuring out how to relate to her students. She had envisioned herself as a friendly older sister to them. One day she overheard a group of her students telling dirty jokes, and she told them a mild one.

About a week later, the vice principal called her to his office to say that parents were outraged about the joke. The student teacher went on to tell of a series of meetings with parents in which she had to explain herself. She described the vice principal's lack of real support during those meetings. Finally she talked about the sobering realization that she had not known where to draw the line with her students. She said, "The dirty joke was horrendous, and I understood that. I understood that I was just trying to be one of the kids, that I felt close to them. . . . I was just being too familiar. I always thought that teaching . . . was relating to the kids."

Stories such as this, in which the student teacher gave a beginning, middle, and end to a segment of her experience, drew characters, presented conflict, and showed how she dealt with it, convey experience in an illuminating and memorable way. (See Mishler, 1986, chap. 4, for an extended discussion of the power of narratives.) If interviewers continually ask a participant to tell a story, the technique will wear out quickly. Used sparingly, however, asking participants to tell stories about particular aspects of their experience can lead to treasured moments in interviewing.

KEEP PARTICIPANTS FOCUSED AND ASK FOR CONCRETE DETAILS

Keep participants focused on the subject of the interview. If they begin to talk about current experience in the first interview, try to guide them back to the focus of that interview, which is to provide contextual background from their life story. Although the interviewer must avoid a power struggle, he or she must exercise enough control of the process so that participants respect the structure and individual purpose of each of the three interviews in the series.

Throughout the interviews, but especially in the first two, ask for concrete details of a participant's experience before exploring attitudes and opinions about it. The concrete details constitute the experience; attitudes and opinions are based on them. Without the concrete details, the attitudes and opinions can seem groundless.

DO NOT TAKE THE EBBS AND FLOWS
OF INTERVIEWING TOO PERSONALLY

Watch for an ebb and flow in interviews and try not to take it too personally. In-depth interviewing often surprises participants because they have seldom had the opportunity to talk at length to someone outside their family or friends about their experience. As a result, they may become so engrossed in the first interview that they say things that they are later surprised they have shared (Spradley, 1979). Interviewers often arrive at the second interview thinking what a wonderful interview the first was, only to be surprised that now the participants pull back and are not willing to share as much as before. At this point, interviewers have to be careful not to press too hard for the type of sharing they experienced before. The third interview allows participants to find a zone of sharing within which they are comfortable. They resolve the issue for themselves.

SHARE EXPERIENCES ON OCCASION

There are times when an interviewer's experience may connect to that of the participant. Sharing that experience in a frank and personal way may encourage the participant to continue reconstructing his or her own in a more inner voice than before. Overused, however, such sharing can distort an interview and distract participants from their own experience to the interviewer's. I can remember sharing stories of mine that I thought connected to what the participant was saying and sensing that the participant was impatient for me to stop talking. (For a somewhat different perspective on the amount of interaction that is desirable between interviewer and participant, see Oakley, 1981.)

ASK PARTICIPANTS TO RECONSTRUCT, NOT TO REMEMBER

Avoid asking participants to rely on their memories. As soon as interviewers ask if people remember something, impediments to memory spring up (Tagg, 1985). Ask participants, in effect, not to remember their experience but rather to reconstruct it. Ask directly "What happened?" or "What was your elementary school experience like?" instead of "Do you remember what your elementary school experience was like?"

Interviewers can assume that the participants will be able to reconstruct their experience and thereby avoid many of the impediments to memory that abound. Reconstruction is based partially on memory and partially on what the participant now senses is important about the past event. In a sense, all recall is reconstruction (Thelen, 1989). In interviewing, it is better to go for that reconstruction as directly as possible.

AVOID REINFORCING YOUR PARTICIPANTS' RESPONSES

Avoid reinforcing what your participant is saying, either positively or negatively. A useful training exercise is to transcribe verbatim 5 minutes of an early interview. What sometimes becomes clear is that the interviewer is in the habit of saying "uh huh" or "O.K." or "yes" or some other short affirmative response to almost every statement from the participant. Sometimes interviewers are hardly aware that they are doing it.

On having such reinforcement called to their attention, many new interviewers suggest that there is nothing inappropriate about the practice. They argue that it shows they are listening and being attentive and that participants appreciate knowing that; it keeps them talking. Often, I think, it is a relatively benign controlling mechanism that is difficult to give up.

But interviewers who reinforce what they are hearing run the risk of distorting how the participant responds (Richardson et al., 1965). A more effective and less invasive method is to refer later in an interview to something participants said earlier. (For a more balanced perspective on reinforcements, see Richardson et al., 1965.)

EXPLORE LAUGHTER

Often a participant will say something and then laugh, sometimes because what he or she just said is self-evidently funny. At other times, the laughter may be nervous or ironic, its origin unclear to the interviewer and often worth exploring. For example, when interviewing a female science teacher, I asked her how the fact that there were 10 women in her community college science division of 60 faculty affected her sense of power in the college. I related the question to Rosabeth Moss Kanter's (1977) discussion of numbers and power in her book, *Men and Women of the Corporation*. The participant responded:

> Well, you see this isn't a corporation. I mean, people are not jockeying for position within, and that would make a tremendous difference, I think, if we were really competitive with one another for something, [laugh] it might be a tremendously important factor. But we're not competing for anything. There are very few people who want to, say, go up to the next step, which is division director. I feel I could get elected to division director, if I so chose. [Pause] My sex would not at all interfere. [Pause] It might even be a plus, but, uh, most people here are not interested, it's not a power play situation; we're all retired really [laugh]. (Seidman et al., 1983)

After she finished and I weighed in my mind the juxtaposition of her laughter with what she was saying, I said, "That sounds bitter." In reply, she spoke about the positive and negative aspects in her experience of not being in a highly competitive, upwardly mobile faculty. I did not follow up at that point because I thought doing so might make her defensive. I wrote in my working notes, "laughter?" and came back to it later in the interview.

FOLLOW YOUR HUNCHES

Follow your hunches. Trust your instincts. When appropriate, risk saying what you think or asking the difficult question. Sometimes during an interview, a question will start to form, perhaps first as a vague impression, then as a real doubt. My experience is that it is important to trust those responses, to figure out the question that best expresses them, and to ask it.

During one interview with an intern teacher, I became increasingly uncomfortable. I could not figure out what was bothering me until I realized that the participant was talking positively about his teaching experience in a very formal way but with very little energy. His nonverbal language was contradicting his verbal language. I began to think he was really very unhappy with his teaching, even though he was talking relatively positively about it.

I was very uncomfortable with this hunch, but finally after we were more than two-thirds of the way into the second interview, I said to him, "You know, I can't figure this out. You are talking as though you are enjoying your teaching, but something about the way you are talking makes me think you are not. Is that fair?"

He responded as though I had opened a floodgate. He began to talk about how angry he was that intern teachers got all the "lowest" classes. He said that even though he had solid math preparation, he would not have a chance to teach upper-level courses for perhaps 5 more years, because all course assignments were made on the basis of seniority. Then he talked about how hard he worked, how little time he had on weekends to be with his wife, and how little money he was making. As a result of following up on a hunch, I gained a completely different picture of his experience, and in the rest of the interview his verbal and nonverbal language coincided.

USE AN INTERVIEW GUIDE CAUTIOUSLY

Some forms of interviewing depend on an interview guide. The interviewers arrive with preset questions to which they want answers or about which they want to gather data. In-depth interviewing, however, is not designed to test hypotheses, gather answers to questions, or corroborate opinions. Rather, it is designed to ask participants to reconstruct their experience and to explore their meaning. The questions most used in an in-depth interview follow from what the participant has said.

Nonetheless, in-depth interviewers may want to develop an interviewing guide. The basic structure of the interview is the question that establishes the focus of each interview in the series. However, interviewers never come into an interview situation as clean slates. They have interests, or they would not have chosen the research topic they did. In addition, some participants will require more prompting than others to go forward in the reconstruction of their experience. Also, over the course of a number of interviews, the interviewer may notice that several participants have highlighted a particular issue, and the interviewer may want to know how other participants have responded to that issue.

For these reasons, in our study of the experience of student teachers we developed a guide that listed the following areas: student teachers' relationship with mentors, with students, with other student teachers, with parents, with tracking, testing, and grading. In most cases, student teachers raised these topics on their own as they talked about their teaching experience. In those instances when they did not, and if there was an opportunity to do so without interrupting or diverting a participant's reconstruction of his or her own experience, the interviewer referred to the interview guide and raised an issue that had not been touched upon.

If interviewers decide to use an interviewing guide, they must avoid manipulating their participants to respond to it. They should ask questions that reflect areas of interest to them in an open and direct way, perhaps acknowledging that the question comes more from their own interest than from what the participant has said. Interviewers must try to avoid imposing their own interests on the experience of the participants. Interviewers working with an interview guide must allow for the possibility that what may interest them or other participants may be of little interest to the person being interviewed. Interview guides can be useful but must be used with caution.

TOLERATE SILENCE

Interviewers sometimes get impatient and uncomfortable with silence. They project that discomfort onto their participants. They see pauses as voids and jump into the interview with a quick question to fill the void. A useful exercise is to play back an interview tape and record how much time the interviewer gives the participant to think before he or she jumps in with a question. My experience is that new interviewers think they are waiting a considerable time before asking their next question, but when we go over audiotapes of their interviews, we determine that in reality they are waiting only a second or two. Thoughtfulness takes time; if interviewers can learn to tolerate either the silence that sometimes follows a question or a pause within a participant's reconstruction, they may hear things they would never have heard if they had leapt in with another question to break the silence. (See Mary-Budd Rowe, 1974, on the effect of how much time teachers wait for answers to questions on the quality of students' responses.)

CONCLUSION

There is no recipe for the effective question. The truly effective question flows from an interviewer's concentrated listening, engaged interest in what is being said, and purpose in moving forward. Sometimes an important question will start out as an ill-defined instinct or hunch, which takes time to develop and seems risky to ask. Sometimes the effective question reflects the interviewer's own groping for coherence about what is being said and is asked in a hesitant, unsure manner.

Effective questioning is so context-bound, such a reflection of the relationship that has developed between the interviewer and the participant, that to define it further runs the risk of making a human process mechanical. To some extent, the way interviewers are as people will be the way they are as interviewers. If interviewers are the sort of people who always have to be talking, who never listen, who demand to be the center of attention most of the time, who are really not interested in other people's stories, no matter what procedures they follow in interviewing, those characteristics will probably pervade the interviewing relationship.

The most important personal characteristic interviewers must have is a genuine interest in other people. They must be deeply aware that other people's stories are of worth in and of themselves and because they offer something to the interviewer's experience. With a temperament that finds interest in others, a person has the foundation upon which to learn the techniques of interviewing and to practice its skills.

7

Interviewing
as a Relationship

Interviewing is both a research methodology and a social relationship that must be nurtured, sustained, and then ended gracefully (Dexter, 1970; Hyman et al., 1954; Mishler, 1986). In part, each interviewing relationship is individually crafted. It is a reflection of the personalities of the participant and the interviewer and the ways they interact. The relationship is also a reflection of the purpose, structure, and method of in-depth interviewing. For example, the fact that the participant and the interviewer meet three times over 2 or 3 weeks results in a relationship different from that which would result from a single-interview structure.

Interviewers can try to craft relationships with their participants that are like islands of interchange separate from the world's definitions, classifications, and tensions. However, individual interviewing relationships exist in a social context. Although an interviewer might attempt to isolate the interviewing relationship from that context and make it unique to the interviewer and the participant, the social forces of class, race, and gender, as well as other social identities, impose themselves. Although interviewers may try to ignore these social forces, they tend to affect their relationships with participants nonetheless.

INTERVIEWING AS AN "I–THOU" RELATIONSHIP

In a section of his book that is elegant even in translation, Schutz (1967) explains that one person's intersubjective understanding of another depends upon creating an "I–Thou" relationship. "Thou" is someone close to the interviewer, still separate, but a fellow person. We recognize "Thou," according to Schutz, as another "alive and conscious human being" (p. 164). Implicit in such an "I–Thou" relationship is a shift from the interviewer's seeing the participant as an object or a type, which he or she would normally describe syntactically in the third person. Schutz goes on to say that a relationship in which each person is "Thou" oriented — that is, in which the sense of "Thou-ness" is mutual — becomes a "We" relationship.

The interviewer's goal is to transform his or her relationship with the participant into an "I–Thou" relationship that verges on a "We" relationship. In the approach to interviewing I have been discussing, the interviewer does not strive for a full "We" relationship. In such a case the interviewer would become an equal participant, and the resulting discourse would be a conversation, not an interview. In an "I–Thou" relationship, however, the interviewer keeps enough distance to allow the participant to fashion his or her responses as independently as possible.

In some approaches to participatory research, however, the interviewers do attempt to create a full "We" relationship (Griffin, 1989). Oakley (1981) argues that not doing so is manipulative and reflects a male, hierarchical model of research. I try to strike a balance, saying enough about myself to be alive and responsive but little enough to preserve the autonomy of the participant's words and to keep the focus of attention on his or her experience rather than mine.

RAPPORT

That balancing act is central to developing an appropriate rapport with the participant. I have never been completely comfortable with the common assumption that the more rapport the interviewer can establish with the participant, the better. Rapport implies getting along with each other, a harmony with, a conformity to, an affinity for one another. The problem is that, carried to an extreme, the desire to build rapport with the participant can transform the interviewing relationship into a full "We" relationship in which the question of whose experience is being related and whose meaning is being made is critically confounded.

In our community college study, one participant invited my wife and me to his house for dinner after the second interview and before the third. I had never had such an invitation from a participant in the study, and I did not quite know what to do. I did not want to appear ungracious, so we accepted. My wife and I went to dinner at his home. We had a wonderful California backyard cookout and it was a pleasure to spend time with the participant and his family. But a few days later, when I met him at his faculty office for the third interview, he was so warm and familiar toward me, that I could not retain the distance that I needed to explore his responses. I felt tentative as an interviewer because I did not want to risk violating the spirit of hospitality that he had created by inviting us to his home.

The rapport an interviewer must build in an interviewing relationship needs to be controlled. Too much or too little rapport can lead to distortion of what the participant reconstructs in the interview (Hyman et al., 1954). For the sake of establishing rapport, for example, interviewers sometimes share their own experience when they think it is relevant to the participant's. Although such sharing may contribute to building rapport, it can also affect and even distort what the participant might have said had the interviewer not shared his or her experience. The interviewing relationship must be marked by respect, interest, attention, and good manners on the part of the interviewer. The interviewer must be constantly alert to what is appropriate to the situation. As in teaching, the interviewing relationship can be friendly but not a friendship. (See Oakley, 1981, for a contrasting perspective.)

At the beginning of an interviewing relationship, I recommend erring on the side of formality rather than familiarity. (See also Hyman et al., 1954). For example, an early step in an interviewing relationship is to ask if the participant minds being called by his or her first name. To do so without asking presumes familiarity, which can be off-putting, especially to older people. Common courtesies such as holding a door, not sitting until the person is seated, and introducing yourself again so that you make sure the participant knows to whom he or she is talking are small steps. But they all add up to expressing respect for the participant, which is central to the interview process.

Once the interview is under way, and as the participant begins to share his or her life history and details of present experience, it is crucial for the interviewer to maintain a delicate balance between respecting what the participant is saying and taking advantage of opportunities to ask difficult questions, to go more deeply into controversial subjects. In our seminar on In-Depth Interviewing and Issues in Qualitative Research, for example, one interviewer said that a participant had made remarks that reflected what the interviewer thought to be racist attitudes. At the time, which was early in her pilot project, the interviewer did not feel comfortable in following up on that aspect of what the participant had said. She hadn't yet developed a technique for exploring such a difficult subject without appearing judgmental. However, by not following up, she later realized that she was left with material which, if used, might be unfair to the participant. She decided that she could not use the *concluding interviews*

material. In future interviews she would find a tactful way to encourage her participants to explore their own words further when she perceived ambiguity in their narrative.

Another reason to control the rapport an interviewer builds in an interviewing relationship is that when the interviews are concluded, the interviewing relationship shifts dramatically. It becomes more distant, less intimate, focusing on what happens to the material generated by the interview. Issues of ownership of the material can easily arise. Interviewers should agree to give a copy of the transcripts or audiotapes to the participant, who has a basic right to these. The participant may want to review the transcripts to see if there is any part with which he or she might not be comfortable and wish to have excluded from the study. This stage of the relationship is likely to be conducted by phone and letter. The rapport an interviewer builds during the interview must be consistent with the relationship the interviewer expects to have with the participant after the interviews are concluded. (See Griffin, 1989, for a model of an active, ongoing relationship between interviewers and participants.)

feedback

Once the interviewer writes a report on the interviews, he or she may share the report with the participants. Lincoln and Guba (1985) refer to such sharing as member-checking, and they indicate that it contributes to the trustworthiness and credibility of the report. But difficult issues can arise at this point. Some interviewers give a right of review to the participant that can amount almost to a veto on how the interviewer works with, analyzes, and writes up the results of the interviewing project. Some researchers go further and suggest that the participant in the interview should also become a participant in working with the material (Griffin, 1989). The stances researchers take on this issue are wide ranging (Patai, 1987). At one end of the continuum are those who argue for a type of co-ownership. At the other are those who suggest that the relationship ends with the interview, and the only obligations that the writer has are to make sure the participants knew why they were being interviewed and the interviewer has not distorted the spirit of what the participant said.

My practice has been to offer to share with participants any material that concerns them. I especially want to know if in working with the interview data I have done anything that makes them vulnerable, or if I have presented anything that is not accurate. Except with regard to issues of vulnerability or inaccuracy, however, I retain the right to write the final report as I see it. (In her study of high schools, Lightfoot 1983, tells of the awkward situation she encountered when participants in her study disagreed with her interpretations.)

The type of relationship the interviewer anticipates after the interview is concluded affects the nature of the relationship the interviewer nurtures during it. If the interviewer has created a full "We" relationship in the process of the interviewing, then he or she must be prepared to deal with the consequences when the time comes to work with the material generated in an interview and report on it. To establish such a deeply sharing, mutually intimate interviewing relationship and then claim one-sided ownership of the material at the conclusion of the interview may cause problems. On the other hand, an interviewer who is explicit about the rights of the participant before the interview begins, and who controls the distance he or she keeps with the participant, establishes the condition for an equitable relationship when working with the material.

SOCIAL GROUP IDENTITIES AND
THE INTERVIEWING RELATIONSHIP

Issues of equity in an interviewing relationship are affected by the social identities that participants and interviewers bring to the interview. Our social identities are affected by our experience with issues of class, race, and gender, and those social forces interact with the sense of power in our lives (Kanter, 1977). The interviewing relationship is fraught with issues of power — who controls the direction of the interview, who controls the results, who benefits. To negotiate these variables in developing an equitable interviewing relationship, the interviewer must be acutely aware of his or her own experience with them as well as sensitive to the way these issues may be affecting the participants.

Race

In our society, with its history of racism, researchers and participants of different racial backgrounds face difficulties in establishing an effective interviewing relationship. It is especially complex for whites and African-Americans to interview each other, but other interracial pairings can also be problematic (Dexter, 1970; Dollard, 1949; Hyman et al., 1954; Labov, 1972; Reese, Danielson, Shoemaker, Chang, & Hsu, 1986; Richardson et al., 1965). In addition, interviewing relationships between those of the same racial background but of different gender, class, and age can engender tensions that inhibit the full development of an effective interviewing relationship.

That is not to say that individual interviewers and participants cannot to some extent subvert the societal context in which we do our research. Interviewers and participants of good will who are from different racial backgrounds can create a relationship that runs counter to prevailing social currents. Maintaining sensitivity to issues that trigger distrust as well as exhibiting good manners, respect, and a genuine interest in the stories of others can go a long way toward bridging racial barriers.

Such bridging attempts are methodologically important. Although the shared assumptions that come from common backgrounds may make it easier to build rapport, interviewing requires interviewers to have enough distance to enable them to ask real questions and to explore, not to share, assumptions. It would be an unfortunate methodological situation if African-Americans could interview only other African-Americans, Latinos only other Latinos, Asian-Americans only other Asian Americans, Native-Americans only other Native-Americans, and whites only other whites.

In my own experience, I have found that the three-interview structure goes some way toward overcoming the initial distrust that can be present when a white interviews an African-American. The three-interview structure can mitigate tensions in other cross-racial interviewing relationships as well. By returning to the participant three times, an interviewer has the opportunity to demonstrate respect, thoughtfulness, and interest in that individual, all of which can work toward ameliorating skepticism. Nonetheless, my experience is that racial politics can make interracial interviewing, no matter the structure of the interviews and the sensitivity of the interviewers, difficult to negotiate.

Of the 76 faculty and administrative participants we interviewed in our community college study (Seidman et al., 1983), only one terminated the interviews before the series was completed. That participant was a male, African-American administrator at a community college who withdrew near the end of the first interview. At the time, he gave no reason. He just said that he wanted to stop.

I remember the feeling of disappointment as my colleague Sullivan and I left the interview. We searched our minds for what had precipitated his decision. I felt both guilty and disheartened and was on the verge of losing confidence in the interviewing methodology. Later, as I reflected further on the episode, I realized that our interview study had become caught up in the racial history and politics of our society. Perhaps instead of being a failure, our interview method had been working too well. As our participant had spoken of his life history, he had begun to deal with the way racism had played out in his life and his career. I think he found himself speaking more honestly to white interviewers than he cared to (Anderson, Silver, & Abramson, 1988; Cotter, Cohen, & Coulter, 1982). His withdrawing was a loss to us and our study. To some degree, it was the cost our research project had to pay for an inequitable society.

Gender

There is evidence that interviewers and participants of different genders get different interviewing results than do those of the same gender (Hyman et al., 1954). The interviewing relationship that develops when participant and interviewer are different genders can be deeply affected by sexist attitudes and behaviors. All the problems that one can associate with sexist gender relationships can be played out in an interview. Males interviewing female participants can be overbearing. Women interviewing men can sometimes be reluctant to control the focus of the interview. Male participants can be too easily dismissive of female interviewers. Interviewers of both genders can fail to see the possibilities of whole areas of exploration if their perspectives are ideologically laden. Nor are interviews among interviewers and participants of the same gender automatically unproblematic. They can be plagued by the assumption of shared perspectives that are not earned or a sense of competition never stated.

In addition to affecting individual relationships between interviewers and participants, sexism influences the total context of research. Interviewing research itself can be characterized as "soft" research — research not likely to yield "hard" data — and can thereby be minimized by a sexist research community (Callaway, 1981). On another level, Patai (1987) argues that if interviewers use women for their own research ends, no matter how well-intentioned the research study is, the dominant paradigm of a society's exploiting women is supported rather than challenged.

There is also the possibility of sexual exploitation in in-depth interviewing because of the sense of intimacy that can develop. Participants talk about the details of their lives while the interviewer listens attentively. A natural bond of fondness and respect develops as the interviewer and the participant explore the participant's experience. Clearly, it is important for interviewers not to exploit that bond sexually.

In one study, a research assistant told me how she had become attracted to one of her participants as a result of interviewing. She wanted to talk about her feelings and their implications for the interview process. She knew that any connection with the participant outside the interview structure would serve only to distort the interviewing relationship. She was worried that even if she had no outside contact with the participant, her fond feelings were affecting the way she asked questions. (See Hyman et al., 1954, p. 54 for another example of how the cordiality of the interviewing relationship affects the way interviewers ask questions.) It helped when I assured her that her feelings were reasonable, but I also emphasized the importance of staying focused on the purpose of the interviews.

It is possible for male and female interviewers and participants to subvert the gender-role stereotypes sexist society would have them play. Interviewers of both sexes can study transcripts of interviews they have done, reconstructing the arrangements they have made to see how they might have employed sexist assumptions in building their interviewing relationships. They can also examine those relationships by reflecting on their interviewing experience in a journal or with a peer. Most important, in the interviewing relationship itself, they can demonstrate a consciousness of sexism and concern for gender equity.

Class, Hierarchy, and Status

When interviewer and participant eye each other through the lens of class consciousness, the stories told and the experiences shared can be distorted (Hyman et al., 1954). A lack of consciousness about class issues can be injurious to both the participant and the interviewer (Sennett & Cobb, 1972).

In a discussion of class in Marxist terms, Patai (1987) described the interviewer as a hybrid of a capitalist and a laborer who is capable of treating the words of participants as commodities to be exploited. If one understands class as a function of status, education, and wealth, interviewers are often middle class and university based, interviewing those who are in some way lower on a scale of status. (Dexter, 1970, runs counter to that notion.)

When we did our study of community college faculty, I became conscious of their sensitivity to the higher education totem pole. In the context of the university, school of education faculty rank low. Some community college faculty participants, however, treated me with either an unwarranted skepticism because of my affiliation with what they perceived as the ivory tower, or an unearned deference because of my affiliation with a university whereas they were "just" in a community college.

Even the use of interviewing itself can be affected by class-based assumptions. For example, Richardson et al. (1965) wrote that participants of "low intelligence, low socio-economic status, or low status in an organized hierarchy may find it difficult to tolerate a preponderance of open questions because they are unused to talking at length spontaneously, articulately, or coherently, or because they are uncomfortable in an unstructured situation" (p. 149). My experience has been that when participants, whatever their class background, place their work in the context of their life histories and are given the space to tell their stories, they can respond to open-ended questions. On the other hand, when class, gender, or racial tension pervades the interviewing relationship, participants are likely to be tight-lipped and restricted in their responses (Labov, 1972; Patton, 1989).

Some interviewers have a wider range of class versatility than others. Given their own life histories, they are able to operate comfortably with people lower and higher in the class structure than they are. Others' life experience has been so homogeneous that they are comfortable only when they are interviewing participants whose social-class experiences are similar to their own. They are reluctant to interview in settings in which they have little experience or classes of people with whom they have had little contact. That reluctance can sometimes result in a skewed sample of participants being interviewed and a picture of the experience being studied that is narrower than warranted.

Age

In addition to race, gender, and class, the relative ages of the participant and the interviewer may affect the type of relationship that develops between them. Some older participants may feel uncomfortable being interviewed by a young interviewer, especially if they feel that the interviewer places them in a subordinate role (Briggs, 1986). Interviewing participants who are much younger or much older takes a special type of sensitivity on the part of the interviewer. He or she must know how to connect to children or seniors without patronizing them. When class, race, linguistic, and age differences are combined, especially in groups of school-age children, the danger that an interviewer will elicit distorted responses is high (Brenner et al., 1985). But when interviewed skillfully and with consciousness of class, race, and age, children can be thoughtful about their experience in and out of school and are capable of reflection that is informative and compelling (Labov, 1972). (For an example of effective interviewing of young adults, see Cleary, 1990.)

DISTINGUISH AMONG PRIVATE, PERSONAL, AND PUBLIC

Interviewing relationships are also shaped by what the interviewer and participant deem are appropriate subjects to explore in the interview. In considering what is appropriate, interviewers may find it useful to distinguish among public, personal, and private aspects of a participant's life (Shils, 1959). The public aspect is what participants do, for example, at work or at school, in meetings, in classes, in offices where their actions are subject to the scrutiny of others. Interviewers tend to be most comfortable exploring these public aspects of participants' experience.

[handwritten marginalia: personal vs public life, false dichotomy]

Participants' private lives involve matters of intimacy, like aspects of relationships participants do not discuss with outsiders for fear of violating those relationships. Each participant or interviewer may have different boundaries for what he or she considers public, personal, and private. In one interview, I asked a participant to talk more about her engagement, which she had mentioned briefly earlier. She said to me very directly, "That's none of your business."

Participants also have personal lives that bridge their public and private experiences. Personal lives are of at least two basic types. The first is participants' subjective experience of public events. Interviewers tend to feel comfortable exploring that aspect of personal experience. Indeed, that is one of the major functions of interviewing as a research method. The second is participants' experience of events that do not occur in their public lives but in their experience with friends and family away from the workplace or school.

New interviewers tend to be less comfortable exploring experiences in this realm. They often question its relevance to the subject of their study. The dichotomy between what is personal and what is public, however, is often false. What happens in people's personal lives often affects what happens in or provides a context for their public lives and can be useful if tactfully explored in interviewing research.

Sometimes interviewers shy away from exploring areas such as death and illness because they themselves are personally uncomfortable, and they assume the participant is too (Hyman et al., 1954; Rowan, 1981). If a participant mentions topics such as these, however, he or she thinks they are relevant. To ignore them or not to explore how they might relate to the subject of the research may signal to the participant that what is most important to him or her is somehow not important to the interviewer. If the participant has risked mentioning a personal topic, my experience is that it is important to acknowledge it and to explore the relationship between that personal experience and the subject of the inquiry.

AVOID A THERAPEUTIC RELATIONSHIP

At the same time, interviewers must avoid changing the interviewing relationship into a therapeutic one. Many see a similarity between the type of open-ended, relatively nondirective interviewing that I have been discussing in this book and the type of exploration that takes place in psychotherapy. It is essential that research interviewers not confuse themselves with therapists. The goals are different (Kahn & Cannell, 1960). The researcher is there to learn, not to treat the participant. The participant did not seek out the researcher and is not a patient. The researcher will see the participant three times, after which their connection will substantially end. They will not have a continuing relationship in which the researcher takes some measure of ongoing responsibility. Researchers are unlikely to be trained therapists. They should know both their own limits and those imposed by the structure and goal of the interviewing process. Researchers must be very cautious about approaching areas of participants' private lives and personal complexities to which they are ill-equipped to respond and for which they can take no effective responsibility.

But even when researchers exercise such caution, the intimacy that can develop in in-depth interviewing sometimes threatens those limits and a participant may find the interviewing process emotionally troubling (Griffin, 1989). Participants may start to cry in an interview. Interviewers may themselves become upset in the face of a participant's tears and not know what to do. My experience is that many times the best thing to do is nothing. Let the participant work out the distress without interfering and taking inappropriate responsibility for it. On the other hand, if the distress continues, the interviewer then has the responsibility to pull back from whatever is causing it.

In my mind, a key to negotiating potentially troubled waters is to assess how much responsibility the interviewer can effectively take in navigating them. In one interview, a participant referred repeatedly to a colleague's nervous breakdown. As much as I was interested in the subject, I did not follow up on it because the participant's repeated references to it troubled me. We were near the end of the third interview. I was not planning to return to the participant's campus the next week. I would not be able to follow up if exploring the topic caused the participant emotional distress. One boundary I learned to observe was the one that marked where I could take effective responsibility for follow-up and where I could not. *Can you follow-up? No? then don't ask!*

RECIPROCITY

The issue of reciprocity in the interviewing relationship can be troubling. The more the interviewing relationship is charged with issues of race, class, and gender, the more complicated the problem of reciprocity can be. Patai (1987) in her study of Brazilian women, most of whom were poor, agonized over what could be perceived as inequity in her research. She wrote a book (Patai, 1988) based on her findings and gained the benefits that usually accrue from such publication. On the other hand, she felt her participants gained little tangible benefit from their cooperation with her. Rowan (1981) talks about the lack of reciprocity that can lead to alienation in research. He sees it as alienation because the researcher is separating participants from their words and then using those words to his or her own ends.

This is the most problematic aspect of interviewing to me. I am sympathetic to the argument that the researcher gets more out of the process than the participant. I know, however, and others write about (Patai, 1987) the type of listening the interviewer brings to the interview. It takes the participants seriously, values what they say, and honors the details of their lives. The reciprocity I can offer in an interview is that which flows from my interest in participants' experience, my attending to what they say, and my honoring their words when I present their experience to a larger public. At the conclusion of the interview I do present my participants with a small gift; but that gift is only a token of my appreciation in the fullest sense of the word *token*. I use it to say thank you and to mark the conclusion of that part of our interviewing relationship. (See Marshall & Rossman, 1989, for a fuller discussion.)

EQUITY

Interviewers and participants are never equal. We can strive to reduce hierarchical arrangements, but usually the participant and the interviewer want and get different things out of the interview. Despite different purposes, researchers can still strive for equity in the process. By equity I mean a balance between means and ends, between what is sought and what is given, between process and product, and a sense of fairness and justice that pervades the relationship between participant and interviewer.

Building equity in the interviewing relationship starts when the interviewer first makes contact with the participant. Equity means the interviewer's going out of his or her way to get the stories of people whose stories are not usually heard. It means the interviewer's not promising what cannot be delivered, and making sure to deliver what is promised. It means being explicit about the purposes and processes of the research. Equity is supported in an explicit written consent form that outlines the rights and responsibilities of the interviewer and the participant in as detailed a manner as reasonable. Equity is involved in scheduling time and place of interviews. Interviewers are asking a great deal of participants. It keeps the process fair when interviewers set up times and places that are convenient to the participant and reasonable for the interviewer.

Equity is also involved in the technique of interviewing. An interviewer who is intrusive, who constantly reinforces responses he or she may like — who is really looking for corroboration of personal views rather than the story of the participant's experience — is not being fair to the purpose of in-depth interviewing. Being equitable in interviewing research means, as we see in Chapter 8, valuing the words of the participant because those words are deeply connected to that participant's sense of worth. Being equitable in interviewing research means infusing a research methodology with respect for the dignity of those we interview.

Researchers cannot be expected to resolve all the inequities of society reproduced in their interviewing relationships, but they do have the responsibility to be conscious of them. Some would argue, though, that research in the social sciences that does not confront these problems contributes to them. (See Fay, 1987, for a review of critical research.) My own sense of the matter is that although it is difficult to do equitable research in an inequitable society, equity must be the goal of every in-depth interviewing researcher. Striving for equity is not only an ethical imperative; it is also a methodological one. An equitable process is the foundation for the trust necessary for participants to be willing to share their experience with an interviewer.

Every step of the interview process can be designed and carried out with the idea of equity in mind. But try as one may to be equitable in interviewing research, equity in interviewing is affected by factors such as racism, classism, and sexism originating outside the individual interviewing relationship or taking place within it. What I have come to grasp over the years I have been doing interviewing research is that the equity of an interviewing relationship, and thereby the quality of the interview, is affected and sometimes seriously limited by social inequities. At the same time, individuals committed to equity in research can find a way first to become conscious of the issues and their own role in them. Then they can devise methods that attempt to subvert those societal constraints. In the process they may end up being able to tell their participants' stories in a way that can promote equity.

8

Working With and Sharing Interview Material

Research based on in-depth interviewing is labor intensive. There is no substitute for studying the interviews and winnowing the almost one million words a study involving 25 participants might yield. (Each series of three interviews can result in 150 double-spaced pages of transcript.)

In planning such a study, allow at least as much time for working with the material as for conceptualizing the study, writing the proposal, establishing access, making contact, selecting participants, and doing the actual interviews. Although there are computer programs that can sort out and combine all the text in which a particular word appears, a computer program cannot produce the connections a researcher makes while studying the interview text. To take full advantage of what interviewing offers, research interviewers must give themselves ample time to study the material they gather.

MANAGING THE DATA

In order to work with the material that interviewing generates, the researcher first has to make it accessible by organizing it. Keeping track of participants through the participant information forms, making sure the written consent forms are copied and filed in a safe place, labeling audiotapes of interviews accurately, managing the extensive files that develop while working with the transcripts of interviews, and keeping track of decision points in the entire process — all require attention to detail, a concern for security, and a system for keeping material accessible. One goal of this administrative work is to be able to trace interview data to the original source on the interview tape at all stages of the research. Another is to be able to contact a participant readily. Misfiling a written consent form from a participant upon whose material a researcher wants to rely heavily can cause a sleepless night.

The best description I have seen of file management for a qualitative research study is in Lofland (1971). Although there is no one right way to organize the research process and the materials it generates, every moment the researcher spends paying attention to order, labels, filing, and documentation at the beginning and in the formative stages of the study can save hours of frustration later.

KEEPING INTERVIEWING AND ANALYSIS SEPARATE

It is difficult to separate the processes of gathering and analyzing data. Even before the actual interviews begin, the researcher often develops an anticipatory frame of mind based on his or her reading and preparation for the study. Once the interviews commence, the researcher cannot help but work with the material he or she is getting. During the interview he or she is processing what the participant is saying in order to keep the interview moving forward. Afterward, the researcher mentally reviews each interview in anticipation of the next one. If the interviewer is working as part of a research team, the team may get together to discuss what they are learning from the process of the interviews.

Some researchers urge that the two stages be integrated so that each informs the other. (See, e.g., Miles & Huberman, 1984; Lincoln & Guba, 1985.) They would have interviewers conduct a number of interviews, study and analyze them, frame new questions as a result of what they have found, and then conduct further interviews.

Although the pure separation of generating and analyzing data is impossible, my own approach is to avoid any in-depth analysis of the interview data until I have completed all the interviews. Even though I sometimes identify topics in early interviews that appear to be salient, I want to avoid imposing meaning from one participant's interviews on the next as best I can. In the work I do, therefore, I first complete all the interviews. Then I study all the transcripts. In that way I try to minimize imposing on the generative process of the interviews what I think I have learned from other participants.

TAPE-RECORDED INTERVIEWS

There is no question in my mind that in-depth interviews must be tape-recorded, although the literature is not unanimous on this point (Bogdan & Taylor, 1975; Briggs, 1986; Hyman et al., 1954; Lincoln &

Guba, 1985; Patton, 1989.) I believe that to work most reliably with the words of participants, the researcher has to transform those spoken words into a written text to study. The primary method of creating text from interviews is to tape-record the interviews and to transcribe them. Each word a participant speaks reflects his or her consciousness (Vygotsky, 1987). The participants' thoughts become embodied in their words. To substitute the researcher's paraphrasing or summaries of what the participants say for their actual words is to substitute the researcher's consciousness for that of the participant. Although inevitably the researcher's consciousness will play a major role in the interpretation of interview data, that consciousness must interact with the words of the participant recorded as fully and as accurately as possible.

There are other benefits to tape-recording as well. By preserving the words of the participant, researchers have their original data. If something is not clear in a transcript, the researchers can return to the source and check for accuracy. Later, if they are accused of mishandling their interview material, they can go back to their original sources to demonstrate their accountability to the data. Tape-recording also benefits the participants. They can feel assured that there is a record of what they have said to which they have access. Thereby they can have more confidence that their words will be treated responsibly. An additional benefit of tape-recording is that interviewers can use the tapes to study their own interviewing technique to improve upon it.

It may seem that the tape recorder could inhibit participants, but my experience is that they soon forget the device. Some interviewers, afraid that a tape-recorder will affect the responses of their participants, use the smallest, least intrusive one they can find. Sometimes they sacrifice audio quality in doing so. It is frustrating to interview someone for 4½ hours and not be able to decipher the audiotape later. I use a tape recorder with a separate microphone because I have found that some recorders with built-in microphones can muffle the sound and make transcribing an agony.

TRANSCRIBING INTERVIEW TAPES

Transcribing interview tapes is time-consuming and potentially costly work. It can be facilitated by using a transcribing machine that has a foot pedal and earphones. Nonetheless it will normally take from 4 to 6 hours to transcribe a 90-minute tape. If possible, the initial transcriptions should be made using a computer-based word-processing program. Later, when researchers sort and refile material, having the interviews in computer files will prove highly efficient and labor saving.

Interviewers who transcribe their own tapes come to know their interviews better, but the work is so demanding that they can easily tire and lose enthusiasm for interviewing as a research process.

Doctoral students ask me if there is a substitute for transcribing the entire interview tape. My response is yes, but not a good one. It is possible to listen to the tapes a number of times, pick out sections that seem important, and then transcribe just those. Although that is a labor-saving approach, it is not a desirable one because it imposes the researcher's frame of reference on the interview data one step too early in the winnowing process. In working with the material it is important that the researcher start with the whole (Briggs, 1986). Preselecting parts of the tapes to transcribe and omitting others tends to lead to premature judgments about what is important and what is not. Once the decision is made not to transcribe a portion of the tape, that portion of the interview is usually lost to the researcher. So although labor is saved in this alternative approach, the cost may be high.

The ideal solution is for the researcher to hire a transcriber. That, however, is expensive and the job must be done well to be worth the effort. Although a transcript can be only a partial representation of the interview (Mishler, 1986), it can reflect the interview as fully as possible by being verbatim. In addition, the transcriber should record all the nonverbal signals such as coughs, laughs, sighs, pauses, outside noises, telephone rings, and interruptions that occur on the tape. A detailed and careful transcript that recreates the verbal and nonverbal material of the interview can greatly enhance the task of a researcher who may be studying the transcript months after the interview occurred.

Note the care and precision with which the following section of an interview audiotape was transcribed. The interviewer is studying what it is like to be a communications major in a large university. Here she is asking the participant about financing her college education:

INTERVIEWER: Uhm, what does that experience mean to you?
PARTICIPANT: The fact that I spent so much money or that my parents like kind of rejected me?
INTERVIEWER: Both.
PARTICIPANT: Uhm, the fact that I spent so much money blows my mind because now I'm so poor and I'm. I can't believe I had so much, I mean I look back [slight pause] to the summer and the fall and [slight pause] I know where my money went. I mean, I was always down the Cape and I'd just spend at least $50 or $60 a night, you know, three or four nights a week. And then when I did an internship in town I was

always driving in town, parking, saying "who cares" and I waitressed three shifts a week so I always had money in my pocket. So it was just, I always had money so, I never really cared and I never prepared for the future or never even considered that my parents wouldn't be there to foot the bill like they'd always been. And I wasn't really aware that they [pause] that they [slight pause and voice lowers] were becoming insulted. (Burke, 1990)

STUDYING AND REDUCING THE TEXT

As one can see, in-depth interviewing generates an enormous amount of text. The vast array of words, sentences, paragraphs, and pages have to be reduced to what is of most importance and interest (McCracken, 1988; Miles & Huberman, 1984). Most important is that reducing the data be done inductively rather than deductively. That is, the researcher cannot address the material with a set of hypotheses to test or with a theory developed in another context to which he or she wishes to match the data (Glaser & Strauss, 1967). The researcher must come to the transcripts with an open attitude, seeking what emerges as important and of interest from the text.

At the same time, no interviewer can enter into the study of an interview as a clean slate (Rowan, 1981). All responses to a text are interactions between the reader and the text (Fish, 1980; Rosenblatt, 1982). That is why it is important that the researcher identify his or her interest in the subject and examine it to make sure that the interest is neither unhealthy nor infused with anger, bias, or prejudice. The interviewer must come to the transcript prepared to let the interview breathe and speak for itself.

Marking What Is of Interest in the Text

The first step in reducing the text is to read it and mark with brackets the passages that are interesting. The best description I have read of this aspect of the winnowing process is Judi Marshall's (1985) "Making Sense as a Personal Process." She acknowledges that what she can bring to the data is her sense of what is important as she reads the transcripts. She expresses confidence in being able to respond to meaningful "chunks" of transcript. She says that she recognizes them when she sees them and does not have to agonize over what level of semantic analysis she is doing. She affirms the role of her judgment in the process. In short, what is required in responding to interview text is no different from what is required in responding to other texts — a close reading plus judgment (Mostyn, 1985).

Marshall also talks about the dark side of this process: that time when, while working with interview data, you lose confidence in your ability to sort out what is important, you wonder if you are making it all up, and you feel considerable doubt about what you are doing. You become worried that you are falling into the trap of self-delusion, which Miles and Huberman (1984) caution is the bane of those who analyze qualitative data. Marshall (1985) calls it an anxiety that you learn to live with.

It is important that the researcher acknowledge that in this stage of the process he or she is exercising judgment about what is significant in the transcript. In reducing the material the interviewer has begun to interpret and make meaning of it. The interviewer-researcher can later check with the participant to see if what he or she marked as being of interest and import seems that way to the participant. Although member-checking can inform the researcher's judgment, it cannot substitute for it (Lightfoot, 1983). That judgment depends on the researcher's experience, both in the past in general and in working with and internalizing the interviewing material; it may be the most important ingredient the researcher brings to the study (Marshall, 1985).

Although I can suggest some of the characteristics that make interviewing texts meaningful to me, there is no model matrix of interesting categories that one can impose on all texts. What is of essential interest is embedded in each research topic and will arise from each transcript. The interviewer must affirm his or her own ability to recognize it.

There are certain aspects of individual experience and social structure to which I respond when they appear. I am alert to conflict, both between people and within a person. I respond to hopes expressed and whether they are fulfilled or not. I am alert to language that indicates beginnings, middles, and ends of processes. I am sensitive to frustrations and resolutions, to indications of isolation and the more rare expressions of collegiality and community. Given the world in which we live, I am sensitive to the way issues of class, race, and gender play out in individual lives, and the way hierarchy and power affect people (Kanter, 1977). I do not, however, come to a transcript looking for these. When they are there, these and other passages of interest speak to me and I bracket them.

Even when working with a research team, I give little instruction about marking what is of interest in a transcript other than to say, "Mark what is of interest to you as you read. Do not ponder about the passage. If it catches your attention, mark it. Trust yourself as a reader. If you are going to err, err on the side of inclusion." As you repeat the winnowing process, you can always exclude material; but materials once excluded from a text tend to become like unembodied thoughts that flee back to the stygian shadows of the computer file. (See Vygotsky, 1987, 210.) Despite the open instruction about marking transcripts, I have found that there is often considerable overlap among my colleagues in what we have marked.

SHARING INTERVIEW DATA: PROFILES AND THEMES

The goal of the researcher in marking what is of interest in the interview transcripts is to reduce and then shape the material into a form in which it can be shared or displayed (Miles & Huberman, 1984). I have used two basic ways to share interview data. First, I have developed profiles of individual participants and grouped them in categories that made sense. Second, I have marked individual passages, grouped these in categories, and then studied the categories for thematic connections within and among them.

Rationale for Crafting Profiles

Although there is no right way to share interview data, and some researchers argue for less reliance on words and more on graphs, charts, and matrices (Miles & Huberman, 1984), I have found that crafting a profile or a vignette of a participant's experience is an effective way of sharing interview data. The idea comes from Studs Terkel's (1972) book *Working*.

Not all interviews will sustain display in the form of a profile. My experience is that only about one out of three interviews is complete and compelling enough to be shaped into a profile that has a beginning, a middle, and an end, as well as some sense of conflict and resolution. Other interviews may sustain what I call a vignette, which is a shorter narrative that usually covers a more limited aspect of a participant's experience.

A profile in the words of the participant is the research product that I think is most consistent with the process of interviewing. We interview in order to come to know the experience of the participants through their stories. We learn from hearing and studying what the participants say. Although the interviewer can never be absent from the process, by crafting a profile in the participant's own words the interviewer allows those words to reflect the person's consciousness.

Profiles are one way to solve the problem the interviewer has of how to share what he or she has learned from the interviews. The narrative form of a profile allows the interviewer to transform this learning into telling a story (Mishler, 1986). Telling stories, Mishler argues, is one major way that human beings have devised to make sense of themselves and their social world. I would add that telling stories is a compelling way to make sense of interview data. The story is both the participant's and the interviewer's. It is in the participant's words, but it is crafted by the interviewer from what the participant has said. (Mishler, 1986, provides an extended discussion of interviewing and its relationship to narratives as a way of knowing, and I strongly recommend it both for his own insights and the further reading that he suggests.) What others can learn from reading a profile of a participant is as diverse as the participants we interview, the profiles we craft and organize, and the readers who read them. I have found crafting profiles, however, to be a way to find and display coherence in the constitutive events of a participant's experience, to share the coherence the participant has expressed, and to link the individual's experience to the social and organizational context within which he or she operates.

Steps in Crafting a Profile

Crafting profiles is a sequential process. Once you have read the transcript, marked passages of interest, and labeled those passages, make two copies of the marked and labeled transcript. (The labeling process is explained later in this chapter.) Using either the capabilities of a word-processing program or a scissors, cut and file the marked passages into folders or computer files that correspond to the labels you devised for each passage. These excerpts will be used in the second, thematic way of sharing material. It is important never to cut up the original transcript because it serves throughout the study as a reference to which the researcher may turn for placing in context passages that have been excerpted.

From the other copy of the transcripts, cut all the passages that you marked as important and paste them together into a single transcript. Your resulting cut-and-paste version may be one-third to one-half the length of the original three-interview transcript.

The next step is to read the cut-and-paste transcript, this time with a more demanding eye. It is very difficult to give up interview material. As you read ask yourself which passages are the most compelling, those that you are just not willing to put aside and underline them. Now you are ready to craft a narrative based on them.

One key to the power of the profile is that it is presented in the words of the participant. I cannot stress too much how important it is to use the first person, the voice of the participant, rather than a third-person transformation of that voice. To illustrate the point for yourself, take perhaps 30 seconds from one of your pilot interviews and craft it into a mini-narrative using the first-person voice of the participant. Then try using your voice and describing the participant in the third person. It should become apparent that using the third-person voice distances the reader from the participant and allows the researcher to intrude more easily than when he or she is limited to selecting compelling material and weaving it together into a first-person narrative.

In creating profiles it is important to be faithful to the words of the participants and to identify in the narrative when the words are those of someone else. Sometimes, to make transitions between passages, you may wish to add your own words. Elsewhere you may want to clarify a passage. Each researcher can work out a system of notation to let the reader know when language not in the interview itself has been inserted. I place such language in brackets. I use ellipses when omitting material from a paragraph or when skipping paragraphs or even pages in the transcripts. In addition, I delete from the profile certain characteristics of oral speech that a participant would not use in writing; for example repetitious "uhms," "ahs," "you knows" and other such idiosyncrasies that do not do the participant justice in a written version of what he or she has said.

If material in interview three fits with a part of the narrative based on interview two, I may decide to edit that material if doing so does not wrench it out of context and distort its meaning. Normally, however, I try to present material in a profile in the order in which it came in the interviews. Material which means something in one context cannot be transposed to another context that changes its meaning. In making all these decisions, I ask myself whether the decisions I am making are fair to the larger interview.

An important consideration in crafting a profile is to protect the identity of the participant if the written consent form calls for doing so. Even when transcribing the interview, use initials for all names that might identify the participant in case a casual reader comes across the transcript. In creating the profile itself, select a pseudonym that does justice to the participant. This is not an easy or a mechanical process. When choosing a pseudonym, take into consideration issues of ethnicity, age, and the context of the participant's life. Err on the side of understatement rather than overstatement. If a participant would be made vulnerable were his or her identity widely known, take additional steps to conceal it. For example, change the participant's geographical location, the details of his or her work — a physics teacher can become a science teacher — and other identifying facets of the person's experience. The extent to which an interviewer needs to resort to disguise is in direct relation to how vulnerable the person might be if identified. But the disguise must not distort what the participant has said in the interview.

The researcher must also be alert to whether he or she has made the participant vulnerable by the narrative itself. For example, Woods (1990) had to exercise extreme caution because if her participants were identified, they might be fired from their teaching positions. Finally, the participant's dignity must always be a consideration. Participants volunteer to be interviewed but not to be maligned or incriminated by their own words. A function of the interviewing process and its products should be to reveal the participant's sense of self and worth.

As an example of a profile, I include here an edited version of one developed by Marguerite Sheehan (1989). (For other examples of such profiles, see Seidman, 1985.) This profile resulted from a pilot study Sheehan conducted of the experience of day-care providers who have stayed in the field for a long time. (See Chapter 3 for a description of her interview structure.)

The participant, Betty, is a family day-care provider. She takes care of six children in her home every day. Most of the children are in "protective slots," that is, their day care is paid for by the state. Their parents are often required to leave them in care because the children either have been or are at risk of being abused or neglected.

The Profile of a Long-Term Day-Care Provider

It's my ninth year [of day care]. It's a long time. I only wanted to do it for a year, see how my daughter would feel about it. . . . I had a different idea of day care. It was more or less like one or two kids come and play. I didn't realize how much work was really involved. But then it became a routine. We eat, we go to the park. There were two ladies in the area who also did child care, that I found out went every morning to the playground. That's how I met a lot of other people. I found out things I never knew before about child care and certain things to do with a certain age. It helped me a great deal with my own daughter. It was good for her. Even then I was taking protective children, so it taught her that not everyone lived the way we did. It helped my husband too. It helped the whole family.

I grew up as an only child [adopted at infancy] but we lived in an apartment house and there was always kids around me. I always took care of kids. . . . My mother never worked. There was that thing with my father: a woman stayed home, takes care of the children and the house. Nothing else, though we could have used the money. I'm sure I bothered my mother a lot of times. She wished she could have gone out and gotten a job instead of staying home with me. But after a while I guess she didn't mind anymore.

[Now] it's funny when kids turn around to me and say, "How come you aren't working? How come you don't have a job?" I try to explain to them, I am working. I'm doing day care. [They say] "No, you don't. How come they are giving you money? You don't even work."

A lot of people [in the neighborhood] know you after a while. "Here comes that lady with all the kids." They know you and help you cross the street. I think they appreciate me but I hear all the time people telling me, "Oh my God, how can you do that? I couldn't do it. Six little kids. God, I'd rather work in a factory!" I do get looks sometimes when I go to the store. I don't care. I couldn't care less. It doesn't bother me.

. . . There are times when I say, "I can't do this anymore. I've got to quit. I'm going crazy." And then you get a child that didn't talk at all when he came, or was really shy and then all of a sudden you get a big hug. That makes me feel good because I know I accomplished something too. Maybe it took a long time but he finally came out of his shell. It makes me feel real good. . . .

Somebody asked me a while back, "Wouldn't you like to do something else? What do you see? What is in the future? You know, no promotions." For me there is a promotion. When a kid comes and finally talks or gives you that big hug or cries by the time they have to leave, it really makes me feel good. That's my promotion. It sounds corny but it's true.

[The children] are not going to be the way you want them to be like, talking or laughing all the time. . . . I had one particular case where the child told me he was going to kick my butt, and he told me how, with a knife! [He said] "That's how you cut up people." He did come back the next day; in his sneakers was a little can opener that you hang on a key chain. He showed it to me. [He said again], "That's how you cut up people." It really scared me. [I thought] this kid has got to go, he's dangerous. But he really isn't. A lot of the time it isn't the kids at all. It's the parents. They [the kids] have to act it out somehow.

I think [day care] a lot of the times really helps the parents. If the child's away for certain hours of the day it gives them a break and hopefully things will go better for them when they realize there is a break. When you get to know the [parent] after a while, sit down and have a cup of coffee, lots of parents sat and cried and told me what happened. Starting from when they were children, or what happened the night before. Sometimes you could really feel for them. . . .

Some protective parents don't really want to deal with me. You can tell. They either don't let me know when the kid is missing; [they say] "So what's the big deal, you don't really need to know." Probably they feel threatened by me. What if the kid does tell me something in the morning that I have to report . . . the parents have needs too. Some of them are really alone. And then I have parents who have kids who weren't abused or neglected. . . . I could say the wrong thing and set them off. I'm not a professional . . .

We have a support group where we meet once a month. The support group consists of four providers and a social worker. We can sit and discuss problems we have with the kids [and ask] what somebody else would do about it. I think that is why a lot of providers quit. Especially the ones who are isolated. There is nobody you can talk to. You talk to little kids all day. It happens to me too. I'll go to a birthday party and I see myself going to the little kids instead of the adults. I feel comfortable there. Sometimes you don't know what to say to adults because you are so alone sometimes. That's why the support group is good. . . . It's only an hour and a half or two hours long, but you hear someone else. Just to sit and talk to another adult makes you feel really good.

I have to keep a log on each of the children. You hear all those things now lately about providers being accused of abusing one of the kids. It really helps to [be able] to go back a couple of months. [To be able to] say, "Wait a minute, this child wasn't even in" [that day] or whatever. That's what I like about a [day care] system too. You can go back and I know they will support you. I mean [if] somebody doesn't know you [after] nine years, they never know you.

. . . when it happened to me, when the parent called me up I felt angry. I think I would have done something very stupid if the person [had been] in the house. It had started off with, "The child is coming home with bruises every day and I want to know" [what's happening]. She was cursing on the phone. And then it got worse. [She said] "My lawyer wants to meet you."

Finally I said, "Look, I've been doing this for such a long time. I've never abused anybody." I was really angry. And I said to myself, "I'm crazy to do this kind of job." I still don't know what happened with the bruises. The bruise was made out to be as though the kid was black and blue from top to bottom. There were two, not even the size of a penny, around the knees. It's probably from crawling. I don't deny the bruises, but I do deny that I'm hurting someone. It did make me angry. I think that's why a lot of people quit. It's just the idea that what if they do believe the other party? What if they close you up? Will they do an investigation? What happens in the meantime?

Maybe I triggered it off because the baby was really sick. I kept telling her to take her to the doctor. I said to the social worker that I want that baby to be seen by a doctor or she doesn't return to day care. It happened on Friday, and Monday I was called. They were threatening me I think, not knowing that I really meant well for the baby, plus for the protection of the other kids.

. . . A few years ago, my husband would have said, "That's it. You've got to quit!" Now he says, "Calm down. They're going to be calm by tomorrow." I can talk to my kids or talk to him. That helps, if you have someone to talk to.

. . . There was one case where I ended up taking the younger child into foster care. I think we would still have her but there were family problems. The father interfering, threatening me, and it became really too much to deal with. When I do see her, I feel awfully bad, like I should have kept her. But we had a choice to make then. [It was] even to the point where my daughter was frightened. She received a call and she got afraid and then we had to make a choice. We couldn't live in fear. I didn't want my daughter to live in fear.

. . . I guess I feel good that several kids really trust me. [They have with me] a place they can come to, a routine. Also they come and tell me certain stuff. [There were] two mothers who felt threatened. One mother stopped by. She told me she had a little bit of a problem with her husband. She sat there where she would never have come before. So it's both children and parents that begin to trust. . . .

My kids all come by bus. It's hard for a kid, being three years old. . . . All of a sudden that big bus comes which is already scary. Your mom puts you on and off you go. You don't know whether you'll ever go home. Some of my kids were in foster care before coming to day care. They don't know if they are going home or not.

It's really hard [when the kids leave family day care]. It try to tell parents to make sure the kid comes on the last day. Plus for a few days I tell the kids that one is going to leave for whatever reason. And then the kid doesn't come back, I don't feel it's right for that child or for the others because nobody knows what's really going on. It's like you rip them out, put them somewhere else and forget about it. I think it's important that the kids do know they are going someplace else. Also, maybe the kids think, "Maybe Betty didn't want him anymore." Maybe the day before I happened to say to him, "You can't do those kinds of things!" And maybe those kids believe that he did something bad so he cannot come here again.

I wish sometimes somebody would call me up and say, "Look I'm going to kill that kid if I can't talk to somebody." . . . Even I had that feeling when my daughter was real small and was going through the thing where she couldn't sleep at night. There were many times I remember sitting in bed having the pillow over my head saying, "Please god, help me. I can't take it anymore." I had the exact same feelings. But then you pull yourself together and you pick up your kid and if she cries three more hours you walk up and down the halls. I think everybody who has kids has had that feeling.

Maybe because of my being adopted, maybe there is something there, that you try to . . . prevent them from getting hurt. . . . As a child it really does bother you. The only thing I could think of was "What was the matter with me?" You see all those cute babies. Who doesn't love a baby? What did I do? Did I scream too much? . . . when I met my real brother, he feels the same way. . . . He said all his life he has had kids around.

. . . I tried other stuff. I went to hairdresser school. I even worked in a factory. I made great money. I've been doing this for the longest time now and I enjoy it. Maybe there is a time when you have to do something else for a while. I'm trying to do stuff after work.

My husband has a different shift. He is glad when he comes home. He likes to stay at home. Me, I'm cooped up in the house. I want to get out. Now we do one weekend with the kids and one weekend we do something [together]. He works in a jail. We sit together. He tells me about the jail. I tell him about day care. We both look at each other and say, "We're crazy. Let's do something. Let's get away."

Sheehan presented a version of this profile to our seminar on In-Depth Interviewing and Issues in Qualitative Research. In her final comments, she wrote,

> Betty had many other things to say that I was not able to fit into this report. She talked quite a bit about how her daughter and husband were involved in the Family Day Care whether through their physical presence or their interest in the children. She told me more stories about individual children and families that she worked with. I was impressed with how she identified at different times with both the children and the parents and how she had to let go while still remaining involved with them. Betty was often nervous and worried that she was not saying the "right thing." She told me that this was the first time that anyone had asked her about the meaning in her work. (Sheehan, 1989)

Betty's profile tells a story in her own words from which anyone interested in day care can learn. As Sheehan goes on with this work, she will interview other long-term day-care providers. If she chooses to do so, she will be able to present a series of profiles grouped together around an organizing topic. In addition to the profiles' speaking for themselves, she will then be able to explore and comment on the salient issues within individual profiles and connections among profiles. For example, in this profile the issues of how people come to the work of day care, the preparation they have, the support they are given, the effect of the low status and genderized nature of the work, the relatively unexplored subject of working with the parents, and the issue of child abuse, to name several, are raised. She will be able to make explicit what she has learned about those subjects through the presentation of Betty's profile and also through connecting Betty's experience to that of others in her sample. By telling Betty's story in her own words, Sheehan is setting the stage for her readers to learn about the issues involved in providing day care through the experiences of a person deeply involved in that work.

MAKING THEMATIC CONNECTIONS

A more conventional way of presenting interview data is to organize excerpts from the transcripts into categories. The researcher then searches for patterns and connections among the excerpts within those categories and for connections between the various categories that might be called themes. In addition to presenting profiles of individuals, the researcher can then present excerpts from the interviews thematically organized.

During the process of reading and marking the transcripts, the researcher can begin to label the passages that he or she has marked as interesting. After having read and indicated interesting passages in two or three participants' interviews, the researcher can pause to consider whether they can be labeled. What is the subject of the passages that are being marked? Are there words or a phrase that seems to describe them, at least tentatively? Is there a word within the passage itself that suggests a category into which the passage might fit? In Sheehan's transcript some of the labels for the passages included might be "background of provider," "support groups," "parents," "impact on family," "abuse," and "parents."

At this point it is important to keep labels tentative. Locking in categories too early can lead to dead ends. Some of the categories will work out. That is, as the researcher continues to read and mark interview transcripts, other passages will come up that seem connected to the same category. On the other hand, some categories that seemed promising early in the process will die out. New ones may appear. Categories that seemed separate and distinct will fold into each other. Others may remain in flux almost until the end of the study (Davis, 1984).

In addition to labeling each marked passage with a term that places it in a category, researchers should also label each passage with a coding system that will designate its original place in the transcript. I use, for example, the initials of the participant, a Roman numeral for the number of the interview in the three-interview sequence, and Arabic numbers for the page number of the transcript on which the passage occurs. Later, when working with the material and considering an excerpt taken from its original context, the researcher may want to check the accuracy of the text and replace it in its full context, even going back to the audiotape itself. The coding of each excerpt allows such retracing.

The next step is to file those excerpts either in computer files under the name of the assigned category or in folders. Some excerpts might fit reasonably into more than one file. Make copies of those and file in the multiple files that seem appropriate.

After filing all the marked excerpts, reread all of them file by file. Start sifting out the ones that now seem very compelling from the ones that seem at this stage to be of less interest. At this point, the researcher is in what Rowan (1981) calls a "dialectical" process with the material (p. 134). The participants have spoken and now the interviewer is responding to their words, concentrating his or her intuition and intellect on the process. What emerges is a synthesis of what the participant has said and how the researcher has responded.

Some commentators regard this sorting and culling as an entirely intuitive process (Tagg, 1985). It is important, however, that researchers also try to form and articulate their criteria for the winnowing and sorting process. By doing so, they give their readers a basis for understanding the process the researcher used in reducing the mass of words to more manageable proportions.

I do not begin to read the transcripts with a set of categories for which I want to find excerpts. The categories arise out of the passages that I have marked as interesting. On the other hand, when I reflect on the types of material that arouse my interest, it is clear that some patterns are present, that I have certain predispositions that I bring with me to my reading of the transcripts.

When working with excerpts from interview material, I find myself selecting passages that connect to other passages in the file. In a way, quantity starts to interact with quality. The repetition of an aspect of experience that was already mentioned in other passages takes on weight and calls attention to itself.

I notice excerpts from a participant's experience that connect to each other as well as to passages from other participants. Sometimes excerpts connect to the literature on the subject. They stand out because I have read about the issue from a perspective independent of my interviewing.

Some passages are told in a striking manner or highlight a dramatic incident. Those are perhaps the most troublesome for me. They are attractive because of their style or the sheer drama of the incident, but I know that I have to be careful about such passages. The dramatic can be confused with the pervasive. The researcher has to judge whether the particular dramatic incident is idiosyncratic or characteristic (Mostyn, 1985).

Some passages stand out because they contradict and seem decisively inconsistent with others. It is tempting to put those aside. These in particular, however, have to be kept in the foreground. The researcher has to try to understand their importance in the face of the other data he or she has gathered (Miles & Huberman, 1984).

The process of working with excerpts from participants' interviews, seeking connections among them, and building interpretative categories is demanding and involves risks. The danger is that the researcher will try to force the excerpts into categories, and the categories into themes that he or she already has in mind, rather than let them develop from the experience of the participants as represented in the interviews. The reason one spends so much time talking to participants is to find out what *their* experience is and the meaning *they* make of it, and then to make connections among the experiences of people who share the same structure. Rowan (1981) stresses the inappropriateness of force-fitting the words of participants into theories derived from other sources.

There is no substitute for total immersion in the data. It is important to try to articulate criteria for marking certain passages as important and selecting some over others in order for the process to have public credibility. It is also important to affirm your judgment as a researcher. You have done the interviewing, studied the transcripts, read the related literature, and mentally lived with and wrestled with the data. As Judi Marshall (1985) says, your feeling of rightness and coherence about the process of working with the data is important. It is your contribution as the researcher.

INTERPRETING AND ANALYZING THE MATERIAL

Interpreting and analyzing are not processes the researcher does only near the end of the project. Marking passages that are of interest, labeling them, and grouping them is interpretative and analytic work. Crafting a profile is an act of interpretation and analysis, as is presenting excerpts arranged in categories.

In some ways, it is tempting to stop at this point, to let the profiles and the categorized excerpts speak for themselves. But one final step in the process is usually called for: asking what you learned from doing the interviews, studying the transcripts, marking and labeling them, crafting profiles, and organizing categories of excerpts. What connections are there among the experiences of the participants you interviewed? What do you understand now that you did not understand before you began the interviews? What surprises have there been? What confirmations of previous instincts? How have your interviews been consistent with the literature? How inconsistent? How have they gone beyond?

Glaser and Strauss (1967) address these questions with a practical suggestion: When you have identified passages that are important but the category in which they fall seems undefined or its significance is unclear, write a memorandum about those passages. Through your writing about them, about how they were picked, about what they mean to you, the properties and import of the category may become clear. If you write such memoranda about each of the categories you have developed and about the profiles you have crafted, the process of writing about them will lead you to discover what it is you find important in them both individually and relatively.

Much of what you learn may be tentative, suggesting further research. In the early stages of our ongoing study of student teachers and mentors (Fischetti, Santilli, & Seidman, 1988; O'Donnell et al., 1989), we began to see evidence in the language of the student teachers we interviewed that tracking in schools was affecting how they were learning to become teachers. That led O'Donnell (1990) to conceptualize a dissertation study on the impact of tracking on learning to become a teacher.

The last stage of interpretation and analysis, then, calls upon the researcher to ask what the research has meant to him or her. In the course of interviewing, the researcher asked the participants what their experience meant to them. Now he or she must respond to the same question. What was the experience like, how do I understand it, make sense of it, see connections in it?

Some of what the researcher learns may lead him or her to propose connections among events, structures, roles, and social forces operating in people's lives. Some researchers would call such proposals "theories" and urge theory building as the purpose of research (Fay, 1987). My own feeling is that although the notion of grounded theory generated by Glaser and Strauss (1967) offered a welcome rationale for qualitative researchers for their inductive approach to research, it also served to inflate the term *theory* to the point that it has lost some of its usefulness.

The narratives we shape of the participants we have interviewed are necessarily limited. Their lives go on; our narratives of them are framed and reified. Betty, whose profile we shared earlier in this chapter, is still working out her relationship to child care. Moreover, the narratives that we present are a function of our interaction with the participants and their words. Although my experience suggests that a number of people reading Betty's transcript would each develop a similar narrative, we still have to leave open the possibility that other interviewers and crafters of profiles would have told a different story. (See Fay, 1987, pp. 166–174.) So, as illuminating as in-depth interviews can be, as compelling as the stories are that they can tell and the themes they can highlight, we still have to bear in mind that Heisenberg's principle of indeterminacy pervades our work, as it does the work of physicists (Polanyi, 1962). We have to allow considerable tolerance for uncertainty (Bronowski, 1973) in the way we report what we have learned from our research.

Every research method has its limits and its strengths. In-depth interviewing's strength is that through it we can come to understand the details of people's experience from their point of view. We can see how their individual experience interacts with powerful social and organizational forces that pervade the context in which they live and work, and we can discover the interconnections among people who live and work in a shared context.

In-depth interviewing has not led me to an easy assessment of the possibilities of progressive reform through research (Bury, 1932; Fay, 1987). It has led me to a deeper understanding and appreciation of the amazing intricacies and, yet, coherence of people's experiences. It has also led me to a more conscious awareness of the power of the social and organizational context of people's experience. Interviewing has provided me with a deeper understanding of the issues, structures, processes, and policies that imbue participants' stories. It has also given me a fuller appreciation of the complexities and difficulties of change. Most important and almost always, interviewing continues to lead me to respect the participants, to relish the understanding that I gain from them, and to take pleasure in sharing their stories.

References

American Anthropological Association. (1983). *Professional ethics: Standards and procedures of the American Anthropological Association*. Washington, DC: Author.

Anderson, B. A., Silver, B. D., & Abramson, P. R. (1988). The effects of the race of the interviewer on race related attitudes of black respondents in SRC/CPS national election studies. *Public Opinion Quarterly, 52*, 289–324.

Applebaum, P. S., Lidz, C. W., & Meisel, A. (1987). *Informed consent: Legal practice and theory*. New York: Oxford University Press.

Bailyn, B. (1963). Education as a discipline. In J. Walton & J. L. Luwethe (Eds.), *The discipline of education* (pp. 126–129). Madison: University of Wisconsin Press.

Becker, H. S., & Geer, B. (1957). Participant observation and interviewing: A comparison. *Human Organization, 16*(3), 28–32.

Bernstein, B. (1975). *Class, codes and control: Vol. 3. Towards a theory of educational transmission*. London: Routledge and Kegan Paul.

Bertaux, D. (Ed.). (1981). *Biography and society: The life history approach in the social sciences*. Beverly Hills, CA: Sage Publications.

Bogdan, R., & Taylor, S. J. (1975). *Introduction to research methods: A phenomenological approach to the social sciences*. New York: John Wiley and Sons.

Brenner, M., Brown, J., & Canter, D. (Eds.). (1985). *The research interview: Uses and approaches*. London: Academic Press.

Briggs, C. L. (1986). *Learning how to ask: A sociolinguistic appraisal of the role of the interview in social science research*. Cambridge: Cambridge University Press.

Bronowski, J. (Narrator). (1973). *Ascent of Man: Knowledge of Certainty, #11* [Film]. Paramus, NJ: Time Life Video.

Burke, K. (1990). The experience of communications majors. Unpublished manuscript, University of Massachusetts, Amherst.

Bury, J. B. (1932). *The idea of progress*. New York: Dover Publications.

Butcher, S. H. (Ed. and Trans.). (1902). *The poetics of Aristotle*. London: MacMillan.

Callaway, H. (1981). Women's perspective: Research as revision. In P. Reason & J. Rowan (Eds.), *Human inquiry* (pp. 457–471). New York: John Wiley and Sons.

Campbell, D., & Stanley, J. (1963). Experimental and quasi-experimental design for research in teaching. In N. L. Gage (Ed.), *Handbook of research on teaching* (pp. 171–246). Chicago: Rand McNally.

Carlisle, L. (1988). Response to literature among first graders: Exploring the possibilities. *Comprehensive Dissertation Index, 1988*, DEV88-13203.

Clark, R. J., & Seidman, I. E. (1988). Retention as a function of pre-service teacher education program design: The MESTEP Case. *Peabody Journal of Education*, 65(2), 79–90.

Cleary, L. M. (1985). *The experience of 11th grade writers: The interaction of thought and emotion in the writing process.* Unpublished doctoral dissertation, University of Massachusetts, Amherst.

Cleary, L. M. (1988). A profile of Carlos: Strengths of a non-standard dialect writer. *English Journal*, 77(1), 59–64.

Cleary, L. M. (1990). The fragile inclination to write: Praise and criticism in the classroom. *English Journal*, 79(2), 22–28.

Cleary, L. M. (in press). *Students struggle for voice* [Working title]. Portsmith, NH: Boynton-Cook of Heinemann Educational Books.

Cotter, P. R., Cohen, J., & Coulter, P. B. (1982). Race-of-interviewer effects in telephone interviews. *Public Opinion Quarterly*, 46, 278–283.

Davis, J. (1984). Data into text. In R. F. Ellen (Ed.), *Ethnographic research: A guide to general conduct* (pp. 295–318). London: Academic Press.

Dean, J. P., and Whyte, W. F. (1958). How do you know the informant is telling the truth? *Human Organization*, 17(2), 34–38.

Department of Health and Human Services. (1981). 45 CFR, Part 46, *Federal Register*, 46(16).

Dexter, L. A. (1970). *Elite and specialized interviewing.* Evanston, IL: Northwestern University Press.

Dollard, J. (1949). *Caste and class in a southern town.* Garden City, NY: Doubleday Anchor Books.

Douglas, J. (1976). *Investigative social research: Individual and team field research.* Beverly Hills, CA: Sage Publications.

Douglas, J. (1985). *Creative interviewing.* Beverly Hills, CA: Sage Publications.

Elbow, P. (1981). *Writing with power.* Oxford: Oxford University Press.

Ellen, R. F. (Ed.). (1984). *Ethnographic research: A guide to general conduct.* London: Academic Press.

Fay, B. (1987). *Critical social science: Liberation and its limits.* Ithaca, NY: Cornell University Press.

Faden, R. B., & Beauchamp, T. L. (1986). *A history and theory of informed consent.* New York: Oxford University Press.

Ferrarotti, F. (1981). On the autonomy of the biographical method. In D. Bertaux (Ed.), *Biography and society: The life history approach in the social sciences.* Beverly Hills, CA: Sage Publications.

Fischetti, J. C., Santilli, S. A., & Seidman, I. E. (1988). *The mask of teacher education reform*. Unpublished manuscript, University of Massachusetts, Amherst.

Fish, S. (1980). *Is there a text in this class?* Cambridge, MA: Harvard University Press.

Frenzy at UMass. (1970, December 21). *Time*, p. 34.

Gage, N. L. (Ed.). (1963). *Handbook of research on teaching*. Chicago: Rand McNally.

Gage, N. L. (1989). The paradigm wars and their aftermath: A "historical" sketch of research on teaching. *Educational Researcher, 18*(7), 4–10.

Galvan, S. (1990). *Experience of minority teachers in local teachers union*. Unpublished manuscript, University of Massachusetts, Amherst.

Gitlin, T. (1987). *The sixties: Years of hope, days of rage*. New York: Bantam Books.

Glaser, B. G., & Strauss, A. S. (1967). *The discovery of grounded theory: Strategies for qualitative research*. New York: Aldine De Gruyter.

Gove, P. B. (Ed.). (1971). *Webster's third new international dictionary of the English language, unabridged*. Springfield, MA: G & C Merriam.

Griffin, P. (1989, March 28). *Using participant research to empower gay and lesbian educators*. Paper presented at the American Educational Research Association Annual Conference, San Francisco, CA.

Hardin, C. (1987). Black professional musicians in higher education: A dissertation based on in-depth interviews. *Comprehensive Dissertation Index 1983–1987*, DEU87-10458.

Heron, J. (1981). The philosophical basis for a new paradigm. In P. Reason & J. Rowan (Eds.), *Human inquiry* (pp. 19–35). New York: John Wiley and Sons.

Hyman, H. H., Cobb, W. J., Fledman, J. J., Hart, C. W., & Stember, C. H. (1954). *Interviewing in social research*. Chicago: University of Chicago Press.

James, W. (1947). *Essays in radical empiricism* and *In a pluralistic universe*. New York: Longmans, Green.

Johnson, J. (1975). *Doing field research*. New York: Free Press.

Kahn, R. L., & Cannell, C. F. (1960). *The dynamics of interviewing*. New York: John Wiley and Sons.

Kanter, R. M. (1977). *Men and women of the corporation*. New York: Basic Books.

Kuhn, T. S. (1970). *The structure of scientific revolution* (2nd ed.). Chicago: University of Chicago Press.

Labov, W. (1972). Logic of non-standard English. *Language in the inner city: Studies in black English vernacular* (pp. 201–240). Philadelphia: University of Pennsylvania Press.

Lather, P. (1986a). Issues of validity in open ideological research: Between a rock and a soft place. *Interchange, 17*(4), 63–84.

Lather, P. (1986b). Research as praxis. *Harvard Educational Review, 56*(3), 257–277.

Lightfoot, S. L. (1983). *The good high school: Portraits of character and culture*. New York: Basic Books.

Lincoln, Y. S., & Guba, E. G. (1985). *Naturalistic inquiry*. Beverly Hills, CA: Sage Publications.

Locke, L. (1989). Qualitative research as a form of scientific inquiry in sport and physical education. *Research Quarterly for Exercise and Sport, 60*(1), 1–20.

Locke, L. F., Spirduso, W., & Silverman, S. J. (1987). *Proposals that work: A guide for planning dissertations and grants proposals*. Beverly Hills, CA: Sage Publications.

Lofland, J. (1971). *Analyzing social settings*. Belmont, CA: Wadsworth.

Mannheim, K. (1975). *Ideology and utopia*. New York: Free Press.

Marshall, J. (1981). Making sense as a personal process. In P. Reason & J. Rowan (Eds.), *Human inquiry* (pp. 395–399). New York: John Wiley and Sons.

Marshall, C., & Rossman, G. B. (1989). *Designing qualitative research*. Newbury Park, CA: Sage Publications.

Matson, F. (1966). *The broken image: Man, science, and society*. Garden City, NY: Archer Books.

McCracken, G. (1988). *The long interview*. Beverly Hills, CA: Sage Publications.

Miles, M. B., & Huberman, A. M. (1984). *Qualitative data analysis: A sourcebook of new methods*. Beverly Hills, CA: Sage Publications.

Mishler, E. G. (1979). Meaning in context: Is there any other kind? *Harvard Educational Review, 49*(1), 1–19.

Mishler, E. G. (1986). *Research interviewing*. Cambridge, MA: Harvard University Press.

Mostyn, B. (1985). The content analysis of qualitative research data: A dynamic approach. In M. Brenner, J. Brown, & D. Canter (Eds.), *The research interview: Uses and approaches*. London: Academic Press.

Oakley, A. (1981). Interviewing women: A contradiction in terms. In H. Roberts (Ed.), *Doing feminist research* (pp. 30–61). Boston: Routledge and Kegan Paul.

O'Donnell, J. F. (1990). *Tracking: Its socializing impact on student teachers: A qualitative study using in-depth phenomenological interviewing*. Unpublished doctoral dissertation, University of Massachusetts, Amherst.

O'Donnell, J. F., Schneider, H., Seidman, I. E., & Tingitana, A. (1989, March 2–5). *The complexities of teacher education in a professional development school: A study through in-depth interviews*. Paper presented at annual meeting of the American Association of Teacher Education, Anaheim, CA. (ERIC Document Reproduction Service No. ED 309 153)

Patai, D. (1987). Ethical problems of personal narratives, or, who should eat the last piece of cake? *International Journal of Oral History, 8*(1), 5–27.

Patai, D. (1988). *Brazilian women speak: Contemporary life stories*. [Interviews edited and translated by Daphne Patai]. New Brunswick, NJ: Rutgers University Press.

Patton, M. Q. (1989). *Qualitative evaluation methods* (10th printing). Beverly Hills, CA: Sage Publications.

Polanyi, M. (1958). *Personal knowledge*. Chicago: University of Chicago Press.

Popkowitz, T. S. (1984). *Paradigm and ideology in educational research.* London: The Falmer Press.

Reason, P. (1981). Methodological approaches to social science. In P. Reason & J. Rowan (Eds.), *Human inquiry* (pp. 43–51). New York: John Wiley and Sons.

Reese, S. D., Danielson, W. A., Shoemaker, P. J., Chang, T. K., & Hsu, H-L. (1986). Ethnicity of interviewer effects among Mexican Americans and Anglos. *Public Opinion Quarterly, 50,* 563–573.

Resnik, H. (1972, March 4). Are there better ways to teach teachers? *Saturday Review,* pp. 46–50.

Reynolds, P. D. (1979). *Ethical dilemmas and social science research.* San Francisco: Jossey-Bass.

Reynolds, P. D. (1982). *Ethics and social science research.* Englewood Cliffs, NJ: Prentice-Hall.

Richardson, S. A., Dohrenwena, B. S., & Klein, D. (1965). *Interviewing: Its forms and functions.* New York: Basic Books.

Rosenblatt, L. (1982). The literary translation: Evocation and response. *Theory Into Practice, 21*(4), 268–277.

Rowan, J. (1981). A dialectical paradigm for research. In P. Reason & J. Rowan (Eds.), *Human inquiry* (pp. 93–112). New York: John Wiley and Sons.

Rowe, M. B. (1974). The relationship of wait-time and rewards to the development of language, logic, and fate control: Part II—Rewards. *Journal of research in science teaching, 11*(4), 291–308.

Sartre, J. P. (1968). *Search for a method* (H. E. Barnes, Trans.). New York: Random House.

Schatzkamer, M. B. (1986). Returning women students in the community college: A feminist perspective. *Comprehensive Dissertation Index 1983–1987,* DEU87-01215.

Schuman, D. (1982). *Policy analysis, education, and everyday life.* Lexington, MA: Heath.

Schutz, A. (1967). *The phenomenology of the social world* (G. Walsh & F. Lenhert, Trans.). Chicago: Northwestern University Press.

Seidman, E. (1985). *In the words of the faculty: Perspectives on improving teaching and educational quality in community colleges.* San Francisco: Jossey-Bass.

Seidman, E., Sullivan, P., & Schatzkamer, M. (1983). *The work of community college faculty: A study through in-depth interviews* (Final Report to the National Institute of Education). Washington, DC. (ERIC Document Reproduction Service No. ED 243 499)

Sennett, R., & Cobb, J. (1972). *The hidden injuries of class.* New York: Knopf.

Sheehan, M. (1989). *Child care as a career: A study of long term child care providers.* Unpublished manuscript, University of Massachusetts, Amherst.

Shils, E. A. (1959). Social inquiry and the autonomy of the individual. In D. Lerner (Ed.), *The human meaning of the social science* (pp. 114–157). Cleveland: Meridian Books.

Solsken, J. (1989, May 3). *Micro-macro: A critical ethnographic perspective on classroom reading and writing as a social process*. Remarks presented at the annual meeting of the International Reading Association, New Orleans, LA.

Spradley, J. P. (1979). *The ethnographic interview*. New York: Holt, Rinehart, and Winston.

Steiner, G. (1978). The distribution of discourse. *On difficulty and other essays*. New York: Oxford University Press.

Sullivan, P. (Producer/director), & Seidman, I. E. (Co-director). (1982). *In their own words: Working in the community college* [Film]. Amherst: University of Massachusetts.

Sullivan, P. (Producer/director), & Speidel, J. (Producer/director). (1976). *The Shaker legacy* [Film]. Amherst: University of Massachusetts.

Tagg, S. K. (1985). Life story interviews and their interpretations. In M. Brenner, J. Brown, & D. Canter (Eds.), *The research interview: Uses and approaches*. London: Academic Press.

Terkel, S. (1972). *Working*. New York: Pantheon Books.

Thelen, D. (1989, September 27). A new approach to understanding human memory offers a solution to the crisis in the study of history. *The Chronicle of Higher Education*, pp. B1, B3.

Todorov, T. (1984). *The conquest of America* (R. Howard, Trans.). New York: Harper and Row. (Original work published 1982)

Tremblay, B. (1990). The experience of instructional design. Unpublished manuscript, University of Massachusetts, Amherst.

Trow, M. (1957). Comment on "Participant observation and interviewing: A comparison." *Human Organization, 16*(3), 33–35.

Vygotsky, L. (1987). *Thought and language* (A. Kozulin, Ed.). Cambridge, MA: MIT Press.

Watkins, C. (Ed.). (1985). The American heritage dictionary of *Indo-European roots*. Boston: Houghton Mifflin.

Wideman, J. E. (1990). Introduction to *The souls of black folk* by W. E. B. Du Bois. New York: Random House, First Vintage Books/Library of America Edition.

Williamson, K. (1990). The ivory tower: Myth or reality. *Journal of Teaching in Physical Education, 9*(2), 95–105.

Williamson, K. (1988). *A phenomenological description of the professional lives and experiences of physical education teacher educators*. Unpublished doctoral dissertation, University of Massachusetts, Amherst.

Woods, S. (1990). *The contextual realities of being a lesbian physical educator: Living in two worlds*. Unpublished doctoral dissertation, University of Massachusetts, Amherst.

Young, S. (1990). *ESL teachers and their work — A study based on interviews conducted with teachers of English as a second language*. Unpublished doctoral dissertation, University of Massachusetts, Amherst.

Index

About the Author

I. E. Seidman is a professor of teacher education at the School of Education, University of Massachusetts at Amherst. He is the author of *In the Words of the Faculty: Perspectives on Improving Teaching and Educational Quality in Community Colleges.*